The Psychology of Wor

ABOUT THE AUTHOR

Dr Elizabeth Dunne lectures on Social and Organisational Psychology at the Department of Applied Psychology, University College, Cork. She has taught students taking postgraduate degrees and professional diplomas in a variety of disciplines, (e.g. health and safety at work; human resource management) as well as undergraduates taking their first degree in psychology. She has also delivered workshops and short courses on special topics in applied psychology to professionals from engineering, project management, general management and medical backgrounds. She consults with many semi-state and private companies on a variety of staff development initiatives. Her research focuses on organisational aspects of health care systems in 'reality' and on the Internet, and on individual activism and commitment to state, community and corporate 'citizenship'.

The Psychology of Working Safely

Elizabeth Dunne MSc PhD

University College, Cork

BP

BLACKHALL

Publishing

This book was typeset by
Gough Typesetting Services for
BLACKHALL PUBLISHING
8 Priory Hall
Stillorgan, Co. Dublin
Ireland
e-mail: blackhall@eircom.net
www.blackhallpublishing.com

ISBN: 1 842180 05 3

A catalogue record for this book
is available from the British Library.

Printed in Ireland by
Colour Books Ltd

Contents

For George

Acknowledgements

To John McCarthy, Department of Applied Psychology, for valuable comments on the manuscript as it emerged.

To Mary Mackey for her insightful layperson's view of the whole story.

To Catherine Sanborn who formatted, saved and, above all, retrieved files thus saving my sanity.

To Michael Henry, Chief Inspector at the Health and Safety Authority, Dublin, for permission to use record forms and for useful documentation of all kinds.

To Dan Dineen of the HSA office in Cork for scenarios.

To Mark Rowland of the HSA office in Galway for photographs of hazards from his own collection.

To Noreen Moynihan, Department of Applied Psychology, for her graphic skills and good humoured support.

To Stephanie Dagg, my virtually perfect editor, for bringing the story to an end.

Introduction

This book is essential reading for anyone who wishes to make significant improvements in workplace safety.

The vast majority of accidents at work are predictable and preventable by fairly straightforward and inexpensive measures. Yet, year in, year out, we see similar accidents repeating themselves throughout the workplaces of Ireland. Why is this and what can be done?

For years we have aspired to "humanise" workplaces. To design and organise them to be suitable for real people who work there: people of both sexes, all shapes and sizes, with temporary or permanent disabilities and different capabilities. This need was identified in the risk assessment requirements of the Safety Statement first published by the Health and Safety Authority in 1993. The current skills shortages throughout Europe are now bringing this to the forefront of policies, as there is now seen to be an economic need to ensure there are no barriers to working or keeping people at work. So how do we improve safety and stop these unnecessary accidents?

This book is timely and starts with the simple, yet obvious premise that "if we are to work more safely, we need to understand how people function. Only then can we design systems which are compatible with the psychological nature of the people who are to use them". It describes how real people function under real working conditions.

The author draws together all the relevant information and very succinctly explains the psychology underlying human behaviour, and how this provides the key to why accidents happen. She then shows how this knowledge can be used to prevent accidents occurring in the workplace with very practical examples. It is very firmly within everyone's reach and ability to apply.

The book is clearly written and easily read, not only by professionals, but also by anyone with an interest in workplace health and safety. It is also an enjoyable read and should become a standard text on occupational safety and health.

Dr Sylvia Wood
Deputy Director General
Health and Safety Authority
Dublin.

Chapter 1

The Nature of Accidents

This book is about preventing accidents and occupational injuries by making job locations psychologically safer places in which to work. Very few accidents happen by chance alone.[1] Official enquiries into major accidents show that most arise in the context of particular personal and interpersonal, technological and organisational situations in the workplace.

The following issues have all been identified as critical in creating the conditions from which accidents result:

- inadequate staff training[2]

- the tacit acceptance of dangerous work practices by managers and/or supervisors[3]

- the failure of the designers of equipment to fully understand and allow for the way people process information[4]

---

[1] Accidents arising from storms, a lightening strike, flooding or an earthquake are examples of such chance events. In most cases, these natural occurrences cannot be prevented, although unwise decisions can exacerbate their effects (e.g. deforestation leading to mud slides in floods). Some people argue that even when the timing of natural events is unpredictable, their negative consequences can be minimised by better forward planning. Green, J. (1996) *Risk and Misfortune*. London: UCL Press.

[2] *Report of the Tribunal of Inquiry on the Fire at the Stardust, Artane, Dublin on the 14th February, 1981* (Dublin Stationery Office). The enquiry into the fire at the Stardust Disco in Dublin identified inadequate staff training as one of the factors in this tragedy in which forty-eight people died and many others suffered burn injuries of varying severity, as well as psychological trauma.

[3] Sheen, Mr Justice. *MV Herald of Free Enterprise. Formal Report of Court No. Investigation 8074* (London: Department of Transport, 1987). The practice of setting sail with the bow doors open, which had been allowed to develop over time, was identified by this report as a contributory factor to this ferry disaster.

[4] Air Accidents Investigation Branch (1990) *Report on the Accident to Boeing 737–400 G-OBME near Kegworth, Leicestershire on January 8, 1989*. Department of Transport, Aircraft Accident Report 4/90, London: HMSO. This aeroplane crash, known as the M1 accident, will be examined in Chapters 5 and 6 since certain aspects of it exemplify some of the crucial issues in the psychology of working safely.

- the psychological pressure on managers and employees to cut corners for
  economic and/or 'political' reasons.

Indeed these *post hoc* or 'with hindsight' analyses showed that most of the
accidents were, in effect, 'waiting to happen'. Sooner or later the unsafe behaviours of individual employees, and the unsafe organisational policies and
managerial practices which had developed unchecked over time, combined
with a trigger element such as a technical failure or malfunction. When that
happened an accident was inevitable.

The explosion of the *Challenger* space shuttle,[5] shortly after take-off on
28 January, 1986, with the death of all seven crew members, is an example of
how technical, social and organisational elements can combine to create a
situation which only needed the trigger of particular weather conditions on
the day of the flight to result in a fatal accident. [6]

The official enquiry into the *Challenger* accident showed that certain engineers had been warning of the likelihood of failure of the O-ring seals of
the rocket booster at low temperatures for some time. Design validation testing of the seals had not been done at temperatures below 53°F and, on the
basis of this, two of the engineers recommended that the flight should not
take place until the temperature around the rings had reached this point.
NASA's Launch Commit Criteria stated that no launch should occur at temperatures below 31°F. The temperature at the launch pad on the morning of
the flight was 29°F. Officials controlling the flight, and others with economic
and political interests in the space shuttle, were keen that the flight — which
had already been delayed three times — should go ahead. This was because
the funding of the space programme was under threat. Questions were already being asked about its cost and value for money. Any hint of technological imperfection might lead to a decision being made to cut funds or to
scrap or 'mothball' the programme. Faced with this possibility, flight con-
trollers decided to trust to luck again. The seals had held up to now. Surely
they would continue to hold.

But on the day of the launch the technological fact of the faulty seals, and
the psychological fact of the organisational 'political' pressures on those
making decisions about the flight, combined with the trigger factor of the
temperature at the site at the time of the flight to produce a lethal situation.

---

[5] The website www.ae.utexas.edu/~jlehman/ethics/challenger.htm gives a detailed
account of the technical, organisational and political/financial factors affecting the
Challenger shuttle flight.

[6] Esser, James K. and Lindoerfer, Joanne S. (1989) 'Groupthink and the Space Shuttle *Challenger* Accident: Towards a Quantitative Case Analysis' *Journal of Behavioural Decision Making*, Vol. 2, pp. 167–77. This article offers an interesting analysis of the way in which group dynamics can result in biased thinking when key
decisions are made under the pressure of organisational and political factors.

The temperature was in the danger zone for failure of the seals. The seals failed. Lives were lost. The space agency and its programme were thrown into disarray and the faith of the American public in its technicians and their technical superiority was shaken.

In case we are tempted to dismiss this high profile accident as having no relevance to the day-to-day concerns of the small or medium sized enterprise in which most of us work, let us consider the following scenario for a moment.

> You are the production manager in a medium sized enterprise. There is a rush on to fill an order for a first time customer who has come to you with a very tight deadline. Not only will you get a bonus if you meet this deadline, you stand to win a new long-term contract from this customer if you deliver on time on this order.

> Walking through the production area, you notice three operators with the safety guards on their machines disabled. From experience you know that operating without the safety guard saves precious seconds at a critical stage in the production process.

> You find yourself struggling with the temptation to turn a blind eye — after all it is only just this once. If you win the new order you are sure of a flow of work with jobs for everyone for the rest of the year. You can always get extra tough on safety once this deadline is over, just so people won't get the wrong idea ...

This illustration has a ring that will be familiar to many people. And we can assume that reasoning like this lay behind the decision of the officials to allow *Challenger* to fly on 28 January, 1986. It is this kind of reasoning which time and again allows managers and employees — in large enterprises and in small, in space agencies, on farms and on construction sites — to argue themselves into accepting and behaving in ways which, with hindsight, they can see could only result in an accident sooner or later.

Let's recap on what has been said so far. Most accidents do *not* happen by chance alone. They arise from particular sets of circumstances in the workplace. These circumstances are created by the interaction between the technology being used, the attitudes, beliefs and motivations of the people working there (both managers and employees), and the policies and practices of the organisation, whether these were formally developed or allowed to just evolve over time. Two or more of these elements create the setting that can result in an accident or in its avoidance.

The *Challenger* accident would not have happened if, irrespective of the economic and political considerations, the shuttle's seals had been replaced. Had that been done then despite the trigger factor of the critical temperature level on the day, it would not have resulted in the disaster because the conditions (faulty seals) would not have been present. In this case, as in the case of most accidents, whether prevailing conditions at the site favour or do not favour the actual occurrence of an accident is determined by the long-standing attitudes and actions of the people in the workplace and the culture and policies of the organisation as a whole.

If we can recognise the critical role which the psychological factors of personal attitude, management style and organisational culture play in setting up the conditions which can favour the occurrence of an accident, then we must also recognise that we can take steps to prevent many accidents or at least minimise the negative consequence of those that do occur. Factors outside our influence such as 'Acts of God' and 'bad luck' do not inevitably result in an accident. If safe conditions generally prevail in the workplace — if, for example, people take care by providing and wearing personal protection equipment, developing good housekeeping practices and designing and purchasing production systems which are compatible with how people think and behave — then chance events need not result in disaster.

A case in point would be where a bucket falls from a scaffolding. If people on the site wear safety helmets, as they are required to, then the potential of the bucket to cause injury is minimised, if not neutralised completely.

Given all that has just been said, the key question becomes: *why don't we work safely*? Why do we personally continue taking risks — turning a blind eye to unsafe behaviours and passing by hazards that we could easily correct? As leaders and managers at the organisational level, why do we under-resource safety, conspire with employees in ignoring unsafe work practices and often set a bad example by taking risks ourselves?

There are two kinds of reasons for this. First, some managers and some employees are simply not seriously interested in safety. Discussing safety with these managers and employees usually elicits remarks such as "Why do you think we have insurance ...?" or "Won't I get compensation if anything happens to me?". Managers who take this view seem not to be aware that the major proportion of the *actual* costs of an accident are indirect items that are often also uninsurable. In a research study in the Irish context, Jacobson and Mottair monitored and costed accidents on a case-by-case basis in twenty-five firms. They report a ratio of from 1.5 to 1.11 for direct as against indirect costs arising from accidents in Northern Ireland and the Republic of Ireland respectively.[7] This means that for each £1 of direct cost related to an accident (such as medical fees, the cost of hospitalisation and worker compensation), between £5 (in Northern Ireland) and £11 (in the Republic of Ireland) more has to be paid out by the organisation to cover the indirect costs 'below the waterline' of the accident cost iceberg in Figure 1.1.

---

[7] Jacobson, D. and Mottair, Z. (1997) *The Costs of Poor Safety in the Workplace.* Research Paper No. 21. Dublin: Dublin City University Business School.

Figure 1.1: The accident cost iceberg — direct versus indirect costs

Accident iceberg for all accidents during study period in NI (from Jacobson and Mottair, 1997)

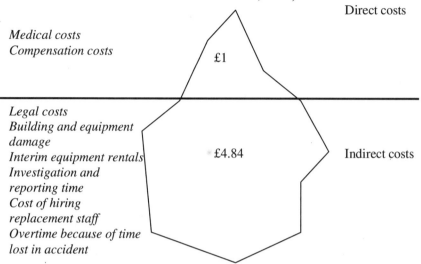

Direct costs

Medical costs
Compensation costs

£1

Legal costs
Building and equipment damage
Interim equipment rentals
Investigation and reporting time
Cost of hiring replacement staff
Overtime because of time lost in accident

£4.84   Indirect costs

Accident iceberg for all accidents during study period in ROI (from Jacobson and Mottair, 1997)

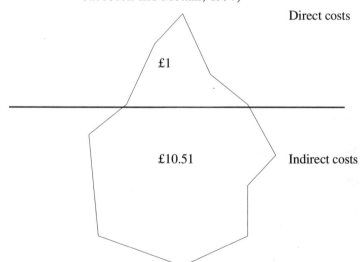

Direct costs

£1

£10.51   Indirect costs

These figures are in line with those found for other countries. [8]

---

[8] Bird, F. E. and Germain, G. L. (1986) *Practical Loss Control Leadership*. International Loss Control Research Institute.

An even more negative picture of the costs associated with accidents at work emerges from a study of the ratio of insurable to uninsurable costs that is included in Jacobson and Mottair's report (see Figure 1.2). Uninsurable costs are a proportion of the direct costs arising from an accident which the organisation must cover from its own financial resources. Work undertaken to prevent a similar accident reoccurring is an example of this kind of cost. (Work of this nature is usually required by the Health and Safety Authority following its inspection of the accident site.) The ratios for Northern Ireland and the Republic of Ireland for insurable to uninsurable costs in £ were 1:10 and 1:28 respectively.

The figures for direct/indirect and insurable/uninsurable costs tell us that managers who cling to the belief that insurance cover will protect them from the adverse financial impact of work related accidents are far from seeing the full picture of the real or *ledger* costs of these events.

A subcategory of this group of managers pleads that business margins are so tight and competition so cut-throat that they "cannot afford" safety. The irony of this position will already be evident to you from the discussion of the Accident Cost Iceberg. The report on loss control from Bird and Germain puts the case for investment in safety even more strongly. They note that the same kinds of factors that create the conditions for a workplace accident also cause many other types of financial loss to the organisation. These losses arise from damage to equipment and the waste of raw materials and other resources. They note that the costs of property damage and waste are often "buried in general maintenance and purchasing costs" (p. 327). Bird and Germain stress that these costs can occur whether or not an injury-accident is involved in the incident or event. The lack of good housekeeping and preventative maintenance, and in particular the unprofessional attitude to managing and giving leadership which underlies these absent behaviours, creates the context for an injury-accident sooner or later. Meanwhile, the organisation loses money because of chronically poor damage and waste control.

Bird and Germain note that the financially significant items are those which, although they may not cost much per capita, "have such a high frequency of repair or replacement that their annual cost to the organisation is critically high" (p. 330). They give an example of a saving of $19,528 over one year for an item which cost only $2 but which was wasted at such a rate that these savings were possible when a programme of waste control was introduced. Bird and Germain also note that the cost-minded manager should consider the price paid for interrupted production, overtime arising from the need to meet a customer deadline and repeat orders lost because of delays resulting from the failure to minimise damage and waste in the workplace. These items of cost also occur, of course, when there is an injury-accident.

Employees who share this short-sighted view of the costs of an accident are assuming that they will make a complete recovery following the event. They are either not considering or are ignoring the possibility of long-term

Figure 1.2: The accident cost iceberg — insured versus uninsured costs

Accident iceberg for all accidents during study period in NI (from Jacobson and Mottair, 1997)

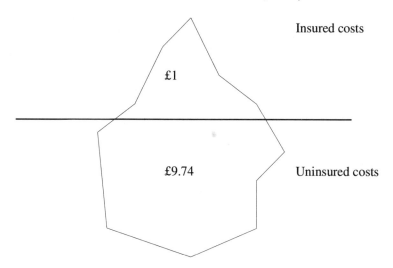

Accident iceberg for all accidents during study period in ROI (from Jacobson and Mottair, 1997)

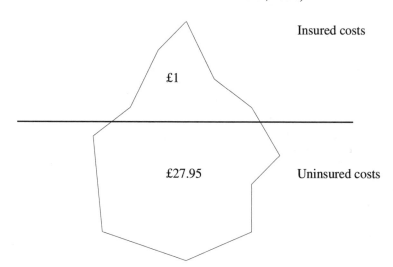

chronic pain, limitation of mobility or other dysfunction, and the effect of this on their quality of life and that of their family.

Even though many employees and managers *are* genuinely interested in safety and in controlling the costs of damaged equipment and wasted resources, they often don't work safely simply because they do not understand their own psychology or the psychology of other people. They, in common with most people, don't really understand what makes them, and other people, 'tick'.

The reason for this is because certain key facts about how people learn from experience, process information under normal and abnormal conditions at work, think and act in group situations, and form and hold attitudes and beliefs about safety and other aspects of their working life are not known, or are misunderstood, by members of those professions who make the significant decisions relevant to safety in our places of work.

If we are to improve safety levels in our workplaces and thus reduce the number and/or seriousness of accidents which occur there, it is crucial that *all* professionals involved with safety at work gain a real understanding and appreciation of the psychological processes which influence the extent to which we all can and will work safely.

The chapters that follow will take you through a range of topics relevant to understanding the psychology of safer working and safety promotion. In the next chapter we look at the very important issue of how our decision about which safety related events to record and the way in which we record them can influence the effectiveness of our risk reduction strategies. This is followed by a chapter on how aspects of the workplace can promote risk taking and the implications that this has for management. Chapter 4 looks at the idea of accident proneness. Chapter 5 considers how people perceive and evaluate risk. The following chapter is on designing for safety. There we look at the relatively new area of cognitive ergonomics and its implications for the design of equipment and production systems in the advanced technology workplace. In the seventh and final chapter we will look at how attitudes are formed and changed and at techniques for promoting safety at work.

Chapter 2

Recording Data to Improve Safety at Work

Creating safer working conditions begins with getting as complete a picture as possible of how hazardous or dangerous the workplace really is. In this regard the employer/manager has a number of options as to what data to record and how to record them. For example, she can decide simply to satisfy statutory requirements to report only those events that must be notified by law. Further she can decide to be satisfied by recording the data on these events as laid out in the official notification forms of the statutory bodies (the Health and Safety Authority in Ireland or the Health and Safety Executive in Britain, for example). On the other hand, the employer/manager may decide to record *all* incidents that have any relevance to safety, and to note all aspects of the work situation with even minimal hazard potential.

In this chapter we examine the consequences for safe working of the strategy for recording safety related data which is decided upon by an organisation.

THE SAFETY STATEMENT

For many people, drawing up the safety statement, as required under Section 12 of the Safety, Health and Welfare at Work Act (1989), will be the first occasion for looking systematically at the hazards of their place of work and the associated risks. A *hazard* is a situation with the potential to give rise to injury to persons, damage to property or damage to the environment — or a combination of these. Technically, *risk* concerns the likelihood of the danger potential of a specific hazard becoming an actuality and the degree of injury and/or damage likely to result from that event. As we shall see in Chapter 5, the process of risk assessment performed by experts differs in quite important ways from the process used by laypersons.

Various techniques for identifying and classifying hazards and assessing their potential to damage people or property to a serious or minor extent, are available in the engineering and technical literature.[1] Guidelines on risk

---

[1] See for example: Rowe, G. (1990) 'Setting Safety Priorities: A Technical and Social

assessment have also been brought out for specific types of hazards[2] and for specific industries.[3]

James Heffernan, an inspector with the Health and Safety Authority (Ireland), has produced a very useful paper on approaches to hazard identification and risk assessment for use by the employer/manager of the small or medium sized enterprise (SME).[4] The methods he suggests are quite straightforward and steer clear of the more complicated quantitative procedures that are better suited to large operations with complex technologies.

In identifying hazards in the SME, Heffernan discusses the use of checklists focusing on different aspects of the workplace. For example, one aspect of a workplace like a hotel would be access. This would include roads and pathways to and from the premises, lobbies, hallways, stairways and steps, lifts and escalators, corridors and doorways. Each of these located in or about the premises would be scrutinised using a checklist drawn up to cover the dangerous element of the particular aspect of access to the hotel. So for example, part of the hazard assessment of a lift would include its weight carrying and space capacity, its conformity to safety standards for lifts, its maintenance requirements and the procedures in the event of an emergency.

Heffernan emphasises that hazard checklists should be specific to the industry or business for which the safety statement is being compiled. Publications from the Irish and British health and safety bodies — the HSA[5] and HSE[6] — can be a useful starting point here. For example, the HSA has published booklets on the hazards associated with farming, forestry, the construction industry, the fishing industry, office work using VDUs, the retail industry and the health services. It also has available a range of information leaflets

Process' in *Occupational Accidents* Vol. 12, pp. 31–40; Bird Jnr, F. E. and Germain, G. L. (1986) *Practical Loss Control Leadership*. The International Loss Control Institute; Steel, C. (1990) 'Risk Estimation' in *Safety Practitioner*. June, 8, (6), pp. 20–21.

[2] *Fire and Explosion Index Hazard Classification Guide*. New York: American Institute of Chemical Engineers (6th edition).

[3] *The Mond Index: How to Identify, Assess and Minimise Potential Hazards on Chemical Plant Units for New and Existing Processes*. (1985) ICI Report Centre Research and Technology Department, PO Box 13, Runcorn Heath, England.

[4] Heffernan, J. (1991) 'Hazard Identification and Risk Assessment for Safety Statements'. Paper delivered to the Seminar on Safety Statements at the University Industry Centre, University College, Dublin 4 on 26 March, 1991.

[5] The Health and Safety Authority, 10 Hogan Place, Dublin 2 regularly produces information leaflets and booklets on the identification and management of specific hazards (e.g. chemicals, noise) and on hazardous aspects of particular industries (e.g. farming).

[6] The publications list of the Health and Safety Executive in Britain is available from the National Industrial Safety Organisation (Ireland) NISO, 10 Hogan Place, Dublin 2. Items from the list may be ordered through NISO.

and booklets on topics such as chemical use in the home and at work and manual handling and lifting, and safety guidelines for use of vehicles in all types of workplaces. From the HSE, publications are available on the hazards associated with spray painting, the leisure industry (fairgrounds, amusement parks, zoos, pop concerts), the offshore energy industry, shift-work and the food industry (butchering and food preparation in kitchens), to name but a random few. The hazards identified in these sector or activity specific publications can be used to draw up a preliminary list of possible hazards for your particular workplace.

Heffernan advocates very strongly that consultation with *all* those who work in the particular industry should be part of the hazard identification process. This is obviously sensible advice and tallies with the multi-disciplinary approach to safety planning advocated by safety researchers.[7] By involving operators, line supervisors and foremen, as well as members of relevant disciplines such as production managers, maintenance personnel, applied psychologists and design engineers at the planning/design stage, the number of aspects of the operation of the system or equipment taken into account is increased. The practical knowledge of operators, line supervisors, foremen and maintenance staff is combined with the theoretical knowledge of the technical specialists and the management skills of the production engineer. Knowledge about how staff are likely to select, evaluate and react to information, and the action they are likely to take under various working conditions, is added by the psychologist. A more complete picture of the technical, operational and human factor related hazards and risks involved in the work situation will result.

Heffernan outlines two methods for estimating the risk associated with hazards based on a paper published in the *Health and Safety Journal* of the National Industrial Safety Organisation (NISO), Ireland. He then suggests a very simple non-quantitative approach that involves allocating each hazard to one of three risk categories:

- the *high risk* category is where the hazard has the potential to cause a fatality or an irreversible injury

- the *medium risk* category involves hazards with the potential to cause a significant but reversible injury

- the *low risk* hazards are those where the potential for injury is slight.

---

[7] See Pidgeon, N. F. (1991) 'Safety Culture and Risk Management in Organisations', *Journal of Cross Cultural Psychology* 22, (1), pp. 129–40. See also Warms-Ringdahl, L. (1987) 'Safety Analysis in Design: Evaluation of a Case Study', *Accident Analysis and Prevention* 19, (4), 305–17.

Jeremy Stranks, a safety and health law expert, has produced two useful guides to the health and safety regulations for Ireland and the United Kingdom.[8] Both guides include explanations of terminology and give checklists that can be used to assess the position of the organisation in terms of compliance with regulations.

The nature, size and complexity of the enterprise are the factors that will influence the approach to hazard and risk assessment that is appropriate in a particular case. As mentioned earlier, methods exist for the assessment of particular types of hazards, such as fires, and of hazards in particular industries, such as the chemical industry. Organisations belonging to a particular industrial or business sector, or those whose area of activity involves specific hazards such as dust or the management of toxic wastes for example, should always refer to their relevant professional, trade or business association and to the local HSA office for guidelines and further information on the hazards concerned.

Systematic approaches to hazard and risk assessment are particularly useful in start-up situations, or where a new technology is being introduced to an established site. Currently, they have been used by many established industries in drawing up their safety statements to comply with the 1989 Act and the regulations arising from it. In all cases they allow for anticipatory planning to avoid accidents and incidents with accident potential.

BUT THAT SHOULDN'T BE THE END OF IT . . .

It may well have struck you that — ironically — the safety statement process may itself be a hazard to safety. The problem is that once the statutory requirement to have a safety statement is met, the statement may be shelved and never looked at again. Having gone through the process once, employers, managers and employees may feel a false sense of security — as if having given some attention to safety and written down principles of good practice was enough to create a safer work environment. Of course nobody rationally believes this. We just act as if we do!

It is *essential* that, once drawn up, the safety statement becomes a real benchmark for the work practices of the organisation. As well as hazard identification and risk assessment, the statement will include specific actions to be taken to remove or neutralise hazards. These may involve equipment modification or redesign, a rota for housekeeping in different parts of the production area, training for personnel and/or the introduction of a 'permit to work' sys-

---

[8] Stranks, J. (1998a) *The Blackhall Guide to Health and Safety in Ireland*, Dublin: Blackhall Publishing; Stranks, J. (1998b) *The Blackhall Guide to Health and Safety in the UK*, Dublin: Blackhall Publishing.

tem. The successful operation of these strategies must be monitored through regular review by the organisation's safety committee or safety representative(s).

It is also essential to carry out a full review of the statement itself on a regular (say biannual) basis. In this way, new hazards, which may be introduced into a workplace through piecemeal changes in technology or work practices, can be identified, their risks assessed and the appropriate action taken to deal with their hazardous potential. In this regard a full safety audit should be part of any programme of *process re-engineering* which a firm might carry out.

SYSTEMS IN CONTEXT AND LEARNING FROM EXPERIENCE

Formal hazard and risk assessments done proactively at start-up, as part of innovation or re-engineering and as part of a full review of the organisation's safety activities, will identify many workplace dangers ahead of time. However, some dangers may lie dormant until the plant or piece of equipment is in operation, or is operating under particular conditions. For example, the problem of 'flutter' with the fan blades in the aeroplane involved in the M1 (Kegworth) air crash in 1989, which was a major factor in the engine failure that led to that crash, could only become evident under actual or simulated flight conditions. Mathematical modelling, which was used to test the upgrade of the thrust of the engine, could not cope with this engineering artefact. This hazard showed up only when the plane was operating in the context of an actual or mechanically simulated flight where the engine was subjected to *real life* stress and strain.

This means that it is not always possible to anticipate *all* of the hazards in a system or piece of equipment at the design stage. Systems or equipment, which may be very adequate or even admirable technical achievements on the engineer's drawing board or CAD screen, may be seriously inadequate, inefficient and even dangerous in a real life work setting. Careful observation, recording and analysis of all events occurring during the commissioning stages of new plant or equipment will give valuable information on real life working. So, too, will analysis of non-accident incidents which occur in the day-to-day working of a particular technology.

In the remainder of this chapter our concern will be with creating a safer work environment by looking at the aspects relevant to safety of these day-to-day events. The events that concern us are of three kinds:

- *incidents* — defined by the British Health and Safety Executive (HSE) as "all undesired circumstances and near misses which have the potential to cause accidents"

- *accidents* — defined by the HSE as "any undesired circumstances which give rise to ill health or injury; damage to property, plant, products or the environment; production losses, or increased liabilities"

- *reportable accidents* — these are accidents, as defined above, which employers are legally required to report to the statutory authority for occupational health and safety. In Ireland and Britain, reportable accidents are those which result in three or more days of lost time for the person(s) involved in the event.

Many managers and employers tend to focus only on reportable accidents when they compile records on the health and safety aspects of their operations. Most will focus on accidents only (those that are not reportable as well as those that are). Few will focus on incidents as well as accidents. Yet the lessons to be learned from the careful analysis of incidents provides managers and employers with one of their best opportunities for improving safety and reducing their accident risk.[9]

To appreciate the power of good incident recording and analysis in creating a safer workplace and reducing the risk of accidents, we need to look at the data collected on the accident to incident ratio.[10] Figure 2.1 illustrates the results of two studies carried out on approximately one million reports of accidents and safety related incidents. Both investigators came up with the 'accident triangle', with which you might already be familiar.

While the details of the two triangles differ, the form of the ratio of fatal and non-fatal accidents to incidents is the same. As you can see, the ratio of accidents involving injury to people and damage to property is proportionately very small relative to the potential for such accidents (incidents) in the workplace. Put another way, there is vastly more danger in the workplace than accident statistics would lead us to believe.

While this state of affairs may be fortunate from the point of view of people who avoid accidents, escaping the worst, as we so often manage to do, is no cause for complacency on the part of the employees or employers. As we saw in Chapter 1, the roots of the majority of accidents lie in the accumulation of casual attitudes and work practices, poor housekeeping and decisions to ignore unsafe behaviours in the workplace made by both managers and employees. Yet singly or in combination, it is these kinds of factors that create the setting favourable to the eventual occurrence of an accident. The 'near miss' incident draws our attention to just these aspects of the work situation.

---

[9] Van Der Shaff, T., Lucas, D. and Hale, A. (1991) *Near Miss Reporting as a Safety Tool*. London: Butterworth/Heinemann.

[10] Heinrich, H.W. (1957) *Industrial Accident Prevention*. New York: McGraw-Hill (5th edition by H.W. Heinrich, D. Petersen and W. Roos, 1980); Bird Jnr, F. E. and Germain, G. L. (1986) *Practical Loss Control Leadership*. The International Loss Control Institute.

Figure 2.1: Accident–incident ratio triangles

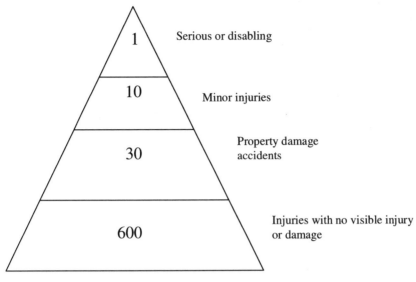

(from Bird and Germain, 1986)

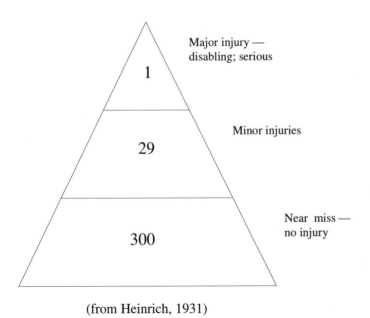

(from Heinrich, 1931)

As noted earlier in this section, hazards may only become evident when the system is operating and work is ongoing. Indeed many *can only* become operative in the real life work context since they have to do with how the work is actually organised and done. If we record and analyse the near miss, we can see what and how we need to change about the way we work in order to reduce the accident potential of our workplace.

Incident analysis actually gives us a more accurate picture of the true danger potential of a workplace than does an analysis of accident statistics. If you look back again at Figure 2.1, you will see that if we concentrate on recording only accidents and so ignore near misses, we get a very different and quite comforting picture of the danger level of most workplaces. Tye noted fifty-four accidents of all types as opposed to four hundred incidents in the reports he studied.[11] We can make the picture even more benign if we concentrate only on reportable accidents — Tye noted just three. Our comfort levels zoom right up if we consider only fatal accidents since their incidence is extremely low.

Focusing exclusively on either accidents, reportable accidents or fatal accidents, or some combination of these three statistics, is not a true reflection of the real state of affairs as regards occupational accident *risk*. Instead they can lull us into a false sense of security, while dangers evident in the near miss accident go unremarked and uncorrected. If we are serious about preventing injury and downtime accidents at work, we must develop ways of recording the information which will give us a proper understanding of the processes by which our particular workplace is made dangerous. To see what this means in practice, let us now look more closely at how reportable accidents and incidents are recorded.

If you study the accident form illustrated in Figure 2.2, it may strike you that it concentrates almost exclusively on the *immediate aspects* of the accident. For example, it asks about who was involved, the date and time of day, and the immediate or proximal aspects of the accident, such as what the injured person was doing at the time of the accident. Information on what went wrong, how the injury occurred and the agent involved in each of these steps is recorded. Details of the injury are recorded, as are the consequences of the accident.

Figure 2.3 is a form of notice of dangerous occurrence.[12]

---

[11] Tye, J. (1976) *Accident Ratio Studies, 1974–1975*. British Safety Council.

[12] The HSE defines a 'dangerous occurrence' as "specified events which may not result in a reportable injury, but have the potential to do significant harm". The difference between a *dangerous occurrence* and a *near miss* as discussed in this book is as follows. I am suggesting that all events with the potential to do harm (*near miss*) be noted. The statutory bodies specify certain events, which they then require to be officially reported to them. This example may help to make this clear. In the HSE *Guidance for Employers in the Healthcare Sector*, the following occurrence is *re-*

Figure 2.2: Form of notice of accident

FORM OF NOTICE OF ACCIDENT

APPROVED UNDER THE SAFETY, HEALTH AND WELFARE AT WORK (GENERAL APPLICATION) REGULATIONS, 1993

(Before completing this form, please see INSTRUCTIONS overleaf)

S.I. No. 44 of 1993

DETAILS OF INJURED PERSON

Name:	Date of birth:		Sex:	Is the injured person:
Address:	Nationality:	Length of Years Months Service:		☐ Employed Full Time ☐ Employed Part Time ☐ Self-employed
	RSI Number:	Date of Accident:	Time of Accident:	☐ A Trainee ☐ A Family Member ☐ A Member of Public
Occupation:	Time of starting work:		Normal time of finishing work:	

EMPLOYER / SELF-EMPLOYED INFORMATION

Name of business or company name:	Phone Number:(2) (+STD Code)	
Address of Head Office:(1)	Nature of Business:	
Address of establishment where injured person was based if different from (1) above:	Approximate no. employed at establishment:	Approximate total no. employed by business:
If accident did not occur at the establishment address state where:		

TYPE OF WORK AND WORK ENVIRONMENT

What type of work was the injured person doing at the time of the accident? (e.g. Iron founding, harvesting, word-processing): _____

Where was the injured person at the time of the accident? (e.g. inside buildings, underground, field, public road, shop etc.) _____

CIRCUMSTANCES OF THE ACCIDENT (An "agent" may be another person, an animal, a substance, equipment or other item)

Briefly describe what the injured person was doing at the time of the accident identifying the agent involved:

Briefly describe the departure from normal, including the agent involved:

Briefly describe the action leading to the injury including the agent which actually caused the injury:

Details of the Injury

Indicate type of injury (tick one box only)		Indicate part of the body most seriously injured (tick one box only)	
☐ Bruising, contusion	☐ Suffocation, asphyxiation	☐ Head, except eyes	☐ Hip joint, thigh, knee cap
☐ Concussion	☐ Gassing	☐ Eyes	☐ Knee joint, lower leg, ankle area
☐ Internal injuries	☐ Drowning	☐ Neck	☐ Foot
☐ Open wound	☐ Poisoning	☐ Back, spine	☐ Toes, one or more
☐ Abrasion, graze	☐ Infection	☐ Chest	☐ Extensive parts of the body
☐ Amputation	☐ Burns, scalds, frostbite	☐ Abdomen	☐ Multiple injuries
☐ Open fracture (i.e. bone exposed)	☐ Effects of radiation	☐ Shoulder, upper arm, elbow	☐ Other
☐ Closed Fracture	☐ Electrical injury	☐ Lower arm, wrist	
☐ Dislocation	☐ Injury not ascertained	☐ Hand	
☐ Sprain, torn ligaments	☐ Other	☐ Fingers, one or more	

CONSEQUENCES OF THE ACCIDENT

Fatal ☐ Non Fatal ☐	Date of resumption of work if back Year Month Day	Anticipated absence if not back	4-7 days ☐ 8-14 days ☐ More than 14 days ☐

DETAILS OF NOTIFIER

Notifier: ☐ Employer/Self Employed ☐ Person in control of workplace ☐ Person Providing Training ☐ Other Date: _____

Address and telephone number for acknowledgement/clarification if different from (1) & (2) above: _____

Signature: _____ Position: _____

Return to Health & Safety Authority, 10 Hogan Place, Dublin 2.   Form No. IR1

INSTRUCTIONS

1. **DETAILS, AS PRESCRIBED OVERLEAF, MUST BE REPORTED TO THE HEALTH AND SAFETY AUTHORITY IN RESPECT OF THE FOLLOWING TYPES OF INCIDENT:-**

    (a) an accident causing loss of life to any employed or self-employed person if sustained in the course of their employment,

    (b) an accident sustained in the course of their employment which prevents any employed or self-employed person from performing the normal duties of their employment for more than 3 calendar days not including the date of the accident,

    (c) an accident to any person not at work caused by a work activity which causes loss of life or requires medical treatment,

2. **THE FOLLOWING CATEGORIES OF PERSON ARE RESPONSIBLE FOR REPORTING ACCIDENTS:**

    (a) employers in the case of the death or injury of employees at work,

    (b) persons providing training in the case of the death or injury of a person receiving training for employment,

    (c) self employed persons in relation to accidents to themselves,

    (d) persons in control of places of work in relation to:
         (i) the work related death or injury of a person not at work,
         (ii) the death of a self employed person,

    (e) the next of kin in the event of the death of a self employed person at a place of work under that person's control.

3. **HOW TO COMPLETE THE FORM**

    The person reporting the accident must only tick one space in each section where option boxes are provided.

    Date of Birth:
    If date of birth of injured person is not available please enter approximate age.

    Employment Status:
    Indicate 'Part-Time' if average hours worked are less than 120 per calendar month, enter 'Full-Time' if they exceed this.

    Occupation:
    If the injured person is an employee or self employed please give sufficient detail to differentiate for example between electricians and fitters or between a nurse or nurses aide.

    Economic Activity:
    The main economic activity being undertaken, e.g. manufacture of computers, road haulage, joinery installation, take away restaurant.

    Work Process and Work Environment:
    This space should indicate the work process carried out by the injured person at the time of the accident and where the injured person was when he/she was injured. Below, two examples are given of how to answer.
    1. Harvesting   Field
    2. Welding   Workshop inside building

    Circumstances of the Accident
    A precise description of the event is to be given under the following three headings:
    a. What the injured person was doing at the time of the accident and for example what person was being attended to, what animal, substance or item was involved or what tool or machine was being used.

    b. What went wrong at the time of the accident. Describe what happened identifying any person, animal, equipment, substance or item involved.

    c. How the person was injured and the person, animal, equipment, substance or item causing the injury.

    Below, two examples are given of the minimum contents of answers.

    Example 1 1. The injured person was **walking** on a **floor.**
                  2. He/She **tripped** over a **hose-pipe.**
                  3. He/She **struck** his/her head against a **table.**

    Example 2 1. The injured person **assisted** a **patient** on the way to the bathroom.
                  2. The **patient stumbled.**
                  3. While **supporting** the **patient** to prevent a fall the injured person's back was strained.

    Details of the Injury
    'Open Wound' includes cuts, lacerations, severed tendons, nerves and blood vessels. 'Burns' includes chemical burns. 'Effects of radiation' includes effects of X-rays, ultravoilet, welding light etc. Forms of injury which are not closely defined such as shock, heatstroke, cardiac arrest should be classified ''other''. ''Electrical Injury'' includes any injury or condition directly due to electric shock.

    Consequences of the Accident
    If injured worker has not yet resumed work please indicate anticipated duration of absence.

    INQUIRIES CONCERNING THIS FORM CAN BE MADE TO THE HEALTH AND SAFETY AUTHORITY (TEL. (01) 6620400) FROM WHICH DETAILED GUIDELINES ARE AVAILABLE.

Figure 2.3: Form of notice of dangerous occurrence

FORM OF NOTICE OF DANGEROUS OCCURRENCE

APPROVED UNDER THE SAFETY, HEALTH AND WELFARE AT WORK (GENERAL APPLICATION) REGULATIONS, 1993

(Before completing this form, please see INSTRUCTIONS overleaf)

S.I. No. 44 of 1993

EMPLOYER / SELF-EMPLOYED INFORMATION

Name of business or company name:	Phone No: (+ STD Code)	
Address of Head Office:	Date of Incident:	
Address of establishment where incident took place if different from above:	Approximate no. employed at establishment:	Approximate total no. employed by business:

TYPE OF WORK BEING UNDERTAKEN AND LOCATION OF DANGEROUS OCCURRENCE

What activity was being undertaken at the time of the incident (e.g. construction, road transport, chemical processing)

Where did the incident take place (e.g. inside buildings, underground, field, public road, shop etc.)

CIRCUMSTANCES OF THE INCIDENT

Description and cause:

DETAILS OF NOTIFIER

| **Notifier:** ☐ Employer/Self Employed   ☐ Person in control of workplace   ☐ Person Providing Training   ☐ Other | Date: |
| Address and telephone number for acknowledgement / clarification if different from above: | Signature: Position: |

Return to Health & Safety Authority, 10 Hogan Place, Dublin 2.

Form No. IR3

INSTRUCTIONS

Where a dangerous occurrence of the kind named below, which is not reportable by reason of death of injury, occurs an employer/self employed person must, as soon as practicable, send a written report in the form overleaf to the Health and Safety Authority.

1. The collapse, overturning, or failure of any load-bearing part of:-

    (a) any lift, hoist, crane, derrick or mobile powered access platform;

    (b) any excavator; or

    (c) any pile-driving frame or rig having an overall height, when operating, of more than seven metres.

2. The explosion, collapse or bursting of any closed vessel, including a boiler or boiler tube, in which the internal pressure was above or below atmospheric pressure.

3. Electrical short circuit or overload attended by fire or explosion which results in the stoppage of the plant involved for more than 24 hours.

4. An explosion or fire occurring in any plant or place which resulted in the stoppage of that plant or suspension of normal work in that place for more than 24 hours, where such explosion or fire was due to the ignition of process materials, their by-products (including waste) or finished products.

5. The sudden uncontrolled release of one tonne or more of highly flammable liquid, liquified flammable gas, flammable gas or flammable liquid above its boiling point from any system, plant or pipe-line.

6. The collapse or partial collapse of any scaffold more than five metres high which results in a substantial part of the scaffold falling or overturning, including, where the scaffold is slung or suspended, a collapse or part collapse of the suspension arrangements (including an outrigger) which causes a working platform or cradle to fall more than five metres.

7. Any unintended collapse or partial collapse of:-

    (a) any building or structure under construction, reconstruction alteration or demolition, or of any false-work, involving a fall of more than five tonnes of material; or

    (b) any floor or wall of any building being used as a place of work, not being a building under construction, reconstruction, alteration or demolition.

8. The uncontrolled or accidental release or the escape of any substance or pathogen from any apparatus, equipment, pipework, pipe-line, process plant, storage vessel, tank, in-works conveyance tanker, land-fill site, or exploratory land-drilling site, which, having regard to the nature of the substance or pathogen and the extent and location of the release or escape, might have been liable to cause serious injury to any person.

9. Any unintentional ignition or explosion of explosives.

10. The failure of any container or of any load-bearing part thereof while it is being raised, lowered or suspended.

11. Either of the following incidents in relation to a pipe-line:-

    (a) the bursting, explosion or collapse of a pile-line or any part thereof;

    (b) the unintentional ignition of anything in a pipe-line, or of anything which immediately before it was ignited was in a pipeline.

12. (1) Any incident in which a container, tank, tank vehicle, tank semi-trailer, tank trailer or tank-container being used for conveying a dangerous substance by road:-

    (i) overturns; or

    (ii) suffers damage to the package or tank in which the dangerous substance is being conveyed.

    (2) Any incident involving a vehicle carrying a dangerous substance by road, where there is:-

    (a) an uncontrolled release or escape from any package or container of the dangerous substance or dangerous preparation being conveyed; or

    (b) a fire which involves the dangerous substance or dangerous preparation being conveyed.

13. Any incident where breathing apparatus while being used to enable the wearer to breathe independently of the surrounding environment malfunctions in such a way as to be likely either to deprive the wearer of oxygen or, in the case of use in a contaminated atmoshpere, to expose the wearer to the contaminant to the extent in either case of posing a danger to his health, but excluding such apparatus while it is being used in a mine or is being maintained or tested.

14. Any incident in which plant or equipment either comes into contact with an overhead electric line in which the voltage exceeds 200 volts, or causes an electrical discharge from such electric line by coming into close proximity to it, unless in either case the incident was intentional.

15. Any accidental collision between a locomotive or a train and any other vehicle at a factory or at dock premses.

16. The bursting of a revolving vessel, wheel, grindstone, or grinding wheel moved by mechanical power.

INQUIRIES CONCERNING THIS FORM CAN BE MADE TO THE HEALTH AND SAFETY AUTHORITY (TEL. (01) 6620400) FROM WHICH DETAILED GUIDELINES ARE AVAILABLE.

Neither of the forms seeks information about the less immediate or distal circumstances that the more detailed reports of accident enquiries have shown to be crucial to understanding the personal, technological, managerial and organisational processes from which accidents arise.

The reason for recording data on an issue like accidents in one particular form rather than another depends upon the use to which the information is to be put. The forms, like those in Figures 2.2 and 2.3, reflect the needs of the agencies that produce them. For example, the HSA in Ireland, the HSE in Britain and the OSHA in the United States of America are statutory bodies set up by their governments to promote and, if necessary, enforce compliance with the provisions of their respective occupational health and safety acts. The format for recording relevant data reflects the necessary preoccupation of these bodies with the question: "Were regulations complied with in this case?". As *enforcement* agencies rather than agencies primarily concerned with safety promotion, these bodies must be more interested in events involving injury or damage, and in the aspects of the immediate situation which can provide evidence as to whether the law was complied with or not. Because of their very particular focus on the legal, regulatory aspects of the workplace, the forms, such as those in Figures 2.2 and 2.3, used by these agencies are not always the most appropriate way of recording information relevant to the creation of safer conditions at work.

Of course this does not mean that we should cease recording or necessarily modify the kind of data currently obtained by the statutory bodies. Apart from the fact of the legal obligation on employers to record these data, information on compliance with regulations for occupational health and safety is a useful barometer of the quality of people's working lives over time and across industries and states. These data can provide useful baseline information against which national and international bodies charged with making public policy in the areas of work and wellbeing can evaluate progress and identify areas needing action. The greater the degree of uniformity of criteria for identifying a reportable incident and recording it between states and statutory organisations, the more direct the comparisons that can be made, and the easier is it for policy makers to assess trends and identify action areas.

This said, it must again be emphasised that relying on the statistical profiles of accidents obtained by state and international agencies in their present

---

portable: "A nurse suffers a needlestick injury from a needle and syringe known to contain Hepatitis B positive blood. The following occurrence is *not reportable*: A domestic suffers a needlestick injury, the source of the sharp is unknown." The near miss perspective sees both events as worthy of examination since the same type of problem is evident in each. By understanding the factors that can give rise to needlestick injuries as such, it should help to reduce the likelihood of their occurrence in general. This in turn reduces the risk of infection where needles and syringes may be infected.

form is not enough if we are serious about accident prevention. If we are to learn from experience, accident records must be kept in a way that will alert the various professionals who use them to the features and trends in the work environment, in staffing levels and staff training, and in organisational and public policy which can contribute to unsafe working.

In the next section we look at one approach to incident/accident root analysis which managers and employers can use to reduce accident risk and create safer working conditions.

INCIDENT/ACCIDENT ROOT ANALYSIS

Figures 2.4 and 2.5 illustrate one approach to getting to the root of situations with hazardous potential in the workplace. Four features are worth emphasising especially:

1. The system involves *long-term* as well as *immediate* action related to the event. In the case of the accident analysed in Figure 2.4, long-term action deals with policy for disposing of and storing redundant or spare furniture.

2. Follow-up, with one *identified person* having the responsibility to monitor the action to be taken and report back to the group, is built into the system.

3. The system is a *no-blame* one, focused on the actions that can be taken to reduce hazards or dangers and facilitate safer working by all in the future.

4. The system aims to be *self-monitoring* and *self-correcting*. Where a similar event has occurred before, it is compared with the current event to see whether they share roots. If they do, reasons why critical factors have not been corrected or why the action taken to correct them has failed are examined. Modifications are made in work practices, equipment or other aspect in the work setting as indicated by the new analysis.

Overcoming Difficulties in Incident Recording

We all want to avoid blame. People also dislike and even fear being seen as sneaks or goody-goods (and other even less complimentary terms!) by their peers. Employees at all levels may fear that if their employer began to see them as 'trouble makers' or 'complainers', their job or promotion prospects would be at risk.[13] As a result many people are reluctant to report incidents. Accidents will probably be noticed since they are more likely to involve some

---

[13]Walters, V. and Haines, T. (1988) 'Workers' Perceptions, Knowledge and Responses Regarding Occupational Health and Safety: A Report on a Canadian Study'. *Social Science Medicine* 27, (11), pp. 1189–96.

Figure 2.4: Incident/accident root analysis

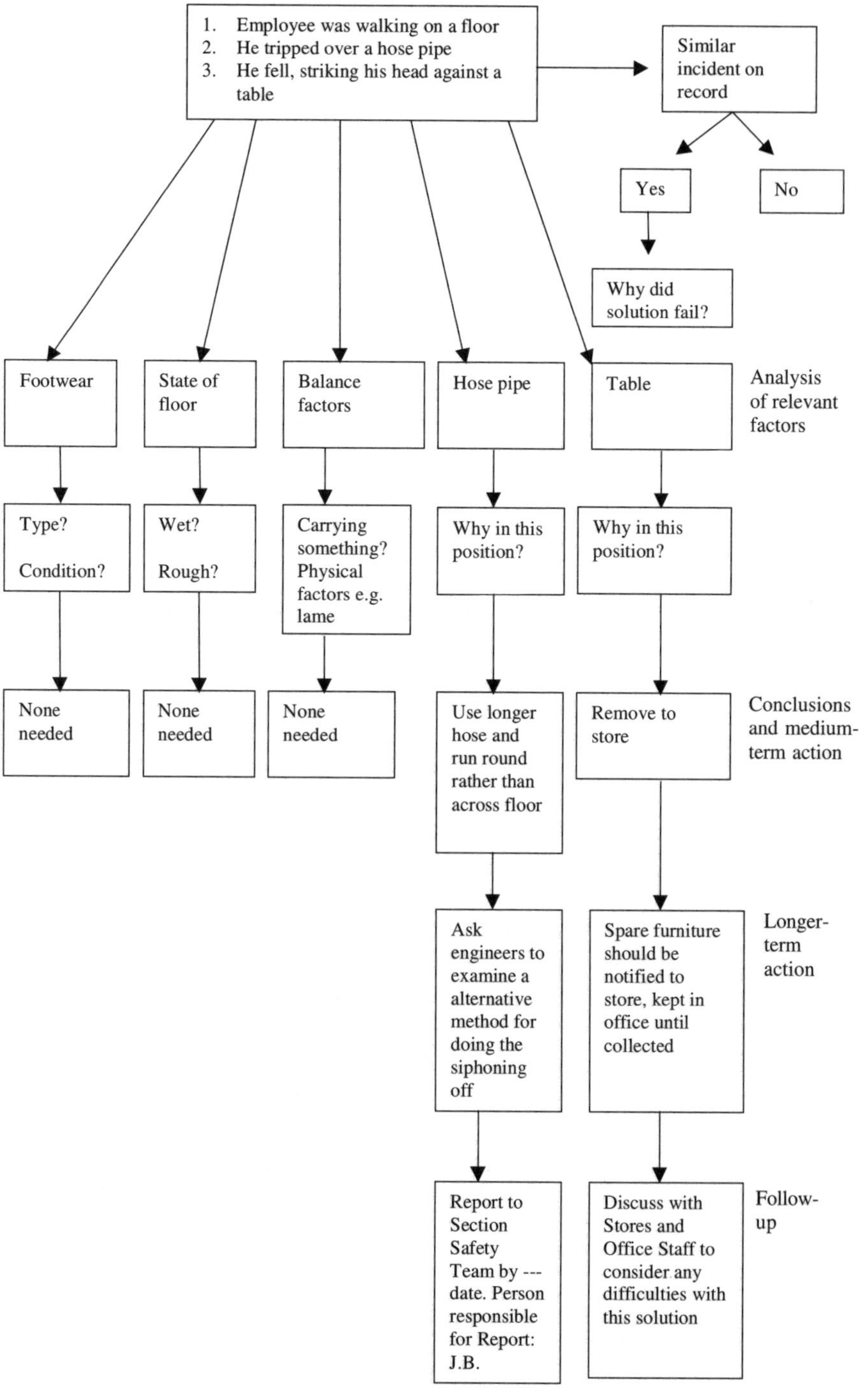

level of disruption to the workflow and/or visible signs of injury or damage.

Given people's understandable (even if not always justified) reluctance to report incidents, how can we get the complete — or nearly complete — picture of the accident potential of our workplace? There are two steps to take. The first step must always be the continuous, visible and genuine effort by employers to create a no-blame learning safety culture. A second pragmatic step can be taken immediately. This is based upon the incident reporting system used by airline pilots in Britain. For much the same reasons as other employees — wishing to avoid blame and fear of being sacked, demoted or not promoted — pilots may prefer not to report incidents in which they are involved when flying. At the same time, they and their professional association recognise the crucial importance of incident reporting if safer flying conditions for themselves and their passengers are to be created. To meet this situation, a confidential incident reporting system has been put in place. Pilots can phone in an account of the incident without identifying themselves. This information is recorded and analysed and used to develop safer procedures and systems in the aeronautics industry.[14]

A similar system could be used by other sectors of industry to get a fuller picture of the hazards of work settings. Confidential reporting would eliminate the fear of blame, embarrassment or ridicule. The incidents reported could be discussed as 'scenarios' at safety meetings and subjected to a root cause analysis, even if only in theory. Action could be taken where appropriate on the basis that "this could happen here".

SUMMING UP

In this chapter we saw that the employer or manager who is serious about safety cannot be satisfied simply with meeting legal requirements in accident recording. Recording only reportable accidents, or accidents and dangerous occurrences, may give a very inaccurate and overly comforting picture of the actual level of danger in a workplace.

Hazard and risk analysis in the case of plant, a business start-up or technological innovation in the workplace is an essential element in promoting safety at work. Regular review of the safety statement is necessary to capture any hazards that may creep in as a result of piecemeal changes in technology or work practices.

Not all hazards can be anticipated at the design stage, and this is especially so where one profession (e.g. systems design engineers, business infor-

---

[14]CHIRP (or the Confidential Human Factors Reports Office) is run by Captain Brian Wilson at the RAF Institute of Aviation Medicine, Farnborough, Hants GU1 4 6SZ.

Figure 2.5: Incident/accident root analysis

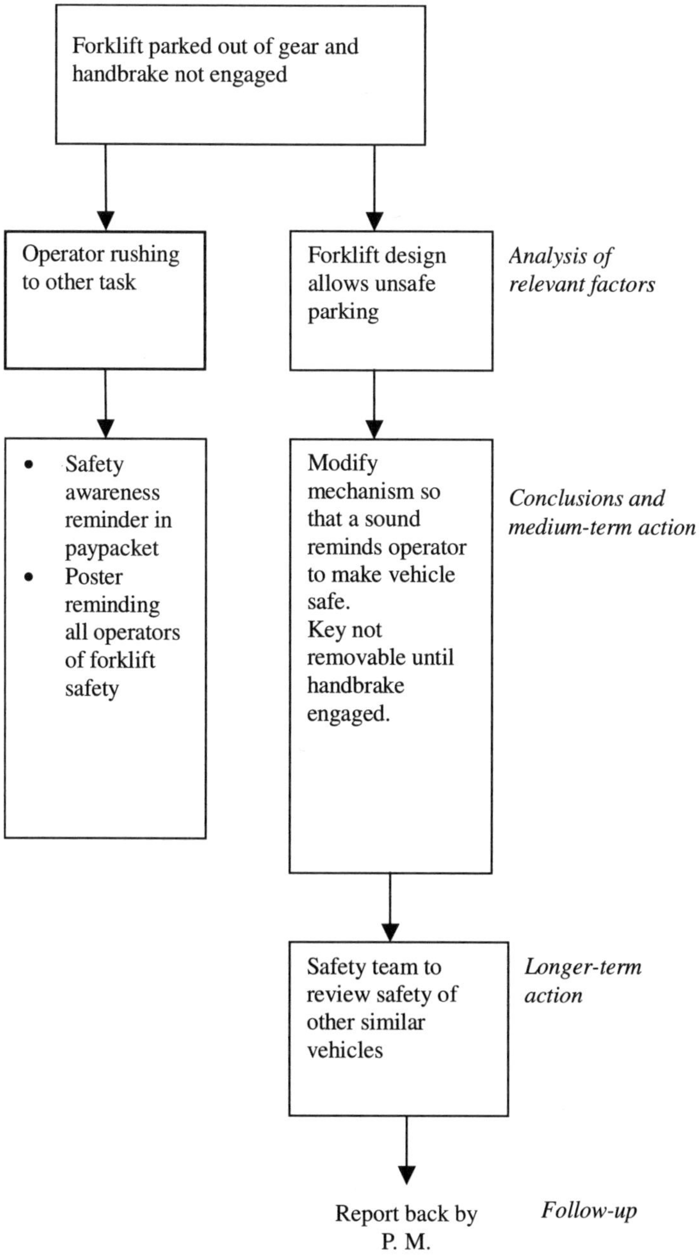

```
┌─────────────────────────────┐
│ Forklift parked out of gear │
│ and handbrake not engaged   │
└─────────────────────────────┘
```

Operator rushing to other task	Forklift design allows unsafe parking	*Analysis of relevant factors*
• Safety awareness reminder in paypacket • Poster reminding all operators of forklift safety	Modify mechanism so that a sound reminds operator to make vehicle safe. Key not removable until handbrake engaged.	*Conclusions and medium-term action*
	Safety team to review safety of other similar vehicles	*Longer-term action*
	Report back by P. M.	*Follow-up*

mation systems consultants) works alone. The number of hazards identified can be increased by inviting the comments of personnel from a variety of operational and applied as well as theoretical backgrounds when the system is being planned.

Finally, hazards which are part of *how* the system is operated and *how* work is done in a particular organisation, and hazards which emerge solely when a system or piece of equipment is in operation, can only be identified by an adequate analysis of accidents and incidents or near misses. In a root cause analysis of accidents and incidents, the aim is to create a no-blame culture where people learn from day-to-day experience. A number of psychological factors, such as peer group pressure and the attitude of some managers to 'complainers', will be a deterrent to the development of this culture in the short term in some cases. While this culture is being created, a confidential incident reporting system can be useful.

Chapter 3

Learning to Take Risks — And What Managers Must do About it

Taking a risk ... and getting away with it — this time

One of the puzzling aspects about behaviour is why we take many of the risks we do. Some people smoke in spite of its link with various serious and life-threatening diseases. Most car drivers have driven without wearing a seatbelt at some time or another. Many routinely drive well above the speed limit. Others have passed cars on blind bends when they could not possibly know whether another vehicle was approaching at speed from the other side. Goggles, helmets and other items of personal protection equipment (PPE) are often not worn at all, or are worn incorrectly, by people at work. And all this in spite of the people involved having the knowledge and ability to behave safely.

HOW WE LEARN TO TAKE RISKS

To understand one aspect of what is going on when people take risks in this way, we must look again at the accident–incident ratio triangles in the last chapter. There we saw that, more often than not, we get away with the risks we take. We may stagger on the loose scaffolding plank but we don't fall this time. We may step back just in time to avoid being sprayed with acid when worn tubing, which has not been preventatively maintained, finally rips open. We may turn our head away just fast enough to avoid a splinter in an eye when machining without wearing goggles.

Because these near misses so rarely result in an injury to ourselves or damage to property, we actually *learn* to take risks at work and elsewhere in our lives. In fact the situation is even more biased towards teaching us to take risks than the accident–incident ratio data indicates.

The pioneer industrial safety researcher Heinrich[1] estimated that the accident–incident triangle was based on a foundation of "550–1,000 or more unsafe acts or exposures to mechanical hazards ... in the average case before even one of the ... narrow escapes from injury occurred" (Heinrich, 1957). Examples of unsafe acts would be failures in housekeeping, like not mopping up the oil that has dripped onto the floor thus creating the conditions for someone to slip, or leaving a bucket where someone could trip over it. Others might be using a blunt headed chisel rather than dressing the head, or not switching off the power take off shaft before dismounting from a tractor.

Because we generally get away with taking these kinds of chances, we learn to go on taking them. While an unsafe act often does not have an immediate consequence in one particular instance, over time these acts are creating the conditions for a possible accident to oneself or others. As we saw in Chapter 1, it is just these kinds of work habits and practices that create the setting favourable to the occurrence of an injury-accident or damage to property.

People learn from experience. If each and every time you touched a badly wired electrical socket you received an electric shock, after just a few such experiences you would obviously avoid handling badly wired electrical equipment and would regularly check all appliances and outlets for signs of wear and repair them promptly. If from the start, and consistently thereafter, an employee *experiences* the danger in the workplace (for example, by actually slipping and falling or by being burned, shocked etc.), there would be no question of accidents arising from unsafe equipment, behaviour or work practices. Heinrich's analysis, and our own experience, shows quite clearly that that is not the case.

---

[1] Heinrich, H. W. (1957) *Industrial Accident Prevention.* New York: McGraw-Hill (5th edition by H. W. Heinrich, D. Petersen and W.Ross, 1980).

Instead we often get away with the chances we take, whether at work or at home, commuting, or in our leisure activities. The psychology of this state of affairs means that we *learn to take chances.* All behaviour is governed by its consequences. Initially the consequences are actual events in the world — actual positive or negative outcomes that follow our actions. Over time, and based upon our experience of the outcomes that our actions have, we build up schemas or scripts about the world. A *schema* is a kind of map or model of what particular aspects of the physical world are like. A *script,* as the term implies, is like the text of a play giving the dialogue that is called for by a particular part or role. These schemas and scripts form the bases for our expectations about the world — about how other people and objects are likely to behave in particular circumstances, about the results which our own actions are likely to have, and the reactions our responses are likely to draw from the people with whom we interact.

Because so much of our unsafe behaviour at work is not followed by a negative outcome, we learn to behave in unsafe ways and to take risks. Our schemas and scripts contain elements that lead us to expect to be safe or invulnerable, often in the face of statistical evidence of a risk of injury or other hazard to our wellbeing. In Chapter 5 we will examine the biases in the way we think and reason about situations which can give rise to these distortions of statistical facts. For now, let's just note what this state of psychological affairs means for safety in the workplace.

WHAT THIS MEANS IN PRACTICE

The practical implications of what has been said so far as regards planning for and promoting greater safety at work are quite straightforward. Firstly they mean that it is generally useless to expect people (including ourselves!) to "be sensible", to "take care" or otherwise respond to exhortations about behaving safely. This is because we do not believe we are in danger.

Psychologically — by which I mean from the point of view of how we process information, and react and act in terms of what we know — we behave moment-to-moment in the ordinary course of our daily lives in terms of what we believe to be the case. What we believe is based upon our own direct experience, or on what we have observed in the relevant experience of others. The pattern of injury and non-injury incidents illustrated in the accident–incident ratio triangle, and in the situation regarding unsafe actions described by Heinrich, is such that our experiences (and observations of the experiences of others) will usually lead us to expect to be safe, no matter what the circumstances. We don't and won't respond to advice and exhortations to take care because *we simply do not believe that we are at risk.* We don't believe we are in danger because our unsafe behaviour has not resulted in a near miss or in injury to ourselves or damage to property in the past. The narrow band approach to accident definition and recording (discussed in Chapter 2) fuels this tendency. It does so by focusing on *harm* rather than on *risk*. Awareness of risk is the crucial factor in improving safety at work. Recording incidents indicates the existence of risk and allows us to identify the hazard which causes it. Removing the hazard, or making it safe, will reduce the incidence of harmful accidents.

Secondly, since negative consequences, which would teach people to act safely and not take chances, so rarely follow their risky behaviour at work, and since exhortations tend to fall on deaf ears, managers generally, and line supervisors in particular, must engineer or organise the work situation so that safety promoting consequences *do* follow unsafe acts and risk taking. Engineering or organising the work environment in this way involves the following steps:

1. *Constant vigilance* on the part of all management staff, and especially line managers and supervisors, for breaches of safety regulations and the occurrence of unsafe acts.

2. *Always* remarking on the unsafe behaviour when it is observed.

3. Advising the person concerned on how to correct unsafe behaviour and *requiring the correct behaviour to be put into practice immediately* or at the earliest practicable opportunity.

4. *Actively promoting safe behaviour* by positively reinforcing instances of it. This means that the manager/supervisor not only comments on unsafe working and requires it to be corrected as soon as possible, but also that he notices when the person is working safely and comments positively on this. In other words, managers/supervisors must be alert and responsive to both sides of the safety coin — they must note and correct unsafe behaviour *and* they must note and positively reinforce safe working behaviour.

5. *Always leading by example* and never cutting corners on safety.

THE PRINCIPLES OF BEHAVIOUR

These steps, which managers must take to engineer an environment where working safely can become the norm, have been shown to be key factors in how people learn practices from experience (as opposed to how they learn theories from books). They are based on the research work of psychologists I. P. Pavlov,[2] B. F. Skinner,[3] E. R. Guthrie[4] and A. Bandura.[5] (You may be

---

[2] Hill, W. F. (1990) *Learning: A Survey of Psychological Interpretations*. 5th edition, New York: Harper & Row. Pavlov's association or connectionist theory of learning is discussed in Chapter 3.

familiar with the story of Pavlov's dogs, and you may also have come across Skinner's work on the reinforcement of behaviour.)

These principles of practical learning don't just apply to learning to work safely. In fact, they apply to *all* areas of behaviour — at work, in the family, at leisure and among friends. Because they are so fundamental to understanding human behaviour right across the spectrum of human action, it is worthwhile taking a closer look at them, and at other principles of learning described by the researchers mentioned above.

We will now look in some detail at the principles of behaviour which relate to the practical problem of creating a safer workplace. To ensure that the links to the practical situations which confront policy makers and managers are clear, the principles of learning will be discussed in the context of a typical safety related scenario in the workplace — in this case a construction site.

A Tale of Two Builders

Tom has upwards of fourteen years' experience as a bricklayer. He has a reputation as a skilled worker. From time to time he is called on by other brickies and by the foreman for his opinion when there is a problem with a job. He takes a pride in this recognition of his experience and expertise.

On Monday morning Tom comes onto a construction site of XX Builders, not wearing his hard hat. Dick, the site foreman, who has been with the company for two weeks, notices this and calls Tom over just as he is starting on a job with Bill, another brickie, and Mick, an apprentice.

Dick shakes his head and says, "For ... sake, Tom. You know you can't be here without a hat. Get it — now."

Dick's reputation in the industry as a stickler on safety has preceded him. Tom knows there is no point in trying to argue with him. He frowns and goes off to the hut for a hat. When he gets

---

[3] Skinner's operant learning approach is discussed in Chapters 6 and 7 of Hill, W. F. (1990) *Learning: A Survey of Psychological Interpretations.*

[4] Guthrie's view of habits and how to change them is discussed in Chapter 4 of Hill, W. F. (1990) *Learning: A Survey of Psychological Interpretations.*

[5] Chapter 11 of Hill (1990) (pages 138–45) discusses Bandura's theory. Bandura focuses on how we learn by observing the behaviour of others. It is the basis for the 'sitting by Nellie' model of training. It also involves learning about the non-technical aspects of work. By noting the consequences which follow someone's actions, we can choose to model our behaviour on theirs (if we want those consequences for ourselves), or try another course of action (if the results have been negative).

back Bill says to him, "You should know your man by now, Tom. Didn't he send Sean off ..."

Tom cuts Bill off. "Enough about it — all right? Let's get on with the job."

Tom is furious with everybody. He is annoyed with Bill for rubbing it in, especially in front of Mick. He is annoyed with Dick for being so fussy and showing him up in front of the other two. He is also annoyed with himself for being caught out by Dick.

Over the next few weeks, when Tom is on Dick's shift he makes sure to wear a hat. He has even been known to turn back for one at the site gate on two occasions when Dick had switched shifts with Harry, the other foreman. Harry is much more easy going on safety. He might or might not mention it if someone wasn't wearing a hat, but he would never send someone off a job to get one.

Dick notices that Tom now always wears a hat on site. On a few occasions he has remarked in passing to Tom that "It is no harm for the young lads to see an old hand like yourself always wearing the hat", or words to this effect.

Tom knows that Dick respects his work and he sees this comment as another acknowledgement of his position on the site. He feels a bit sheepish that he doesn't always wear a hat. If Harry is on and the day is hot he sometimes doesn't bother. After the second time Dick mentions his influence as an example to the apprentices, he begins to wear a hat irrespective of who the shift foreman is. He also begins to take a more general interest in safety on the site.

Meanwhile Mick, the apprentice, who witnessed Tom's earlier embarrassment over the hat, has taken to making sure that he isn't caught out and he always wears a hat. Some months later he moves to another site and no longer works with Tom, Dick and Bill. Nobody on this site is particular about safety. They don't comment negatively if you don't wear a hat and they don't comment positively if you do. Eventually, Mick becomes very casual about it and about other aspects of safety. If working safely takes more time or involves extra effort, he doesn't bother.

The scenario just described covers the main principles of behaviour involved in engineering a safer work environment. They are:

• punishment

• negative reinforcement

• recency effects (doing what you last did) and habit change

• consistency and the way consequences are scheduled

- expenditure of effort

- modelling/imitation effects

- discrimination learning and the stimulus control of behaviour

- positive reinforcement

- extinction.

The Moral of the Story

Let us now look at how each of the principles in the above list operated in this construction site scenario.

Punishment

Being picked out in front of his mates is a *punisher* for Tom. Technically any consequence to an action that has the effect of decreasing the likelihood of that action being repeated in the future is a punisher. Tom won't want the embarrassment of a repetition in front of Bill and Mick or other workmates, so he will be more likely to wear a hat after this experience. Punishment on its own is a very ineffective strategy for producing behaviour change. It tells the person what actions *not* to do but it doesn't indicate what the appropriate or desired actions are. This obviously creates resentment and often anger on the part of the recipient who may feel that the manager/supervisor is playing a kind of 'cat and mouse' game — waiting to pounce on some piece of behaviour but never making it clear what is actually wanted. The bad feeling which is created by a punishing approach to managing safety[6] will often spill over into other areas of work and result in a poor company climate and lack of team spirit overall.[7] It may also be a breeding ground for poor industrial relations.

Negative reinforcment

The possibility of a repetition of the confrontation with Dick acts as a *negative reinforcer* for Tom to wear a hat. Technically a negative reinforcer is a

---

[6] Punishment as a management style is a risky strategy in all areas of management. Actions such as imposing penalties as a *first* or *only* rather than a last resort, sarcasm, humiliation, bullying etc., risk losing the goodwill of employees and pay poor dividends in terms of co-operation, loyalty, productivity and quality of work over time. The 'punishing' management style usually goes along with a 'Theory X' view of employees. This holds that people are lazy and irresponsible and will work only when forced to do so. See McGregor *The Human Side of Enterprise* for more details on this style and its opposite, 'Theory Y'.

[7] McGregor, D. (1960) *The Human Side of Enterprise*. New York: McGraw-Hill.

consequence which people will take action to avoid. It has the effect of getting people to do what they should do. In this case, it has the effect of getting
Tom to wear a hat on site. A key element is his *motivation* to do so. He is not
wearing a hat because it is the safe thing to do. He is wearing it to *avoid* a
threatened punisher become an *actuality*. He wants to avoid another embarrassing confrontation with Dick.

Although negative reinforcement produces a negative motivation for the
safe behaviour, at least it does have the effect of increasing the likelihood of
that behaviour taking place. As you can see, there is a complex link between
punishment and negative reinforcement. A punisher is the actual occurrence
of a negative consequence following some action taken by the person. It has
the effect of *reducing* the likelihood of the person repeating that action in the
future. In our example the punisher is the public dressing down from Dick.
Its effect is to reduce the likelihood of Tom coming onto the site on Dick's
shift without wearing a hat.

A negative reinforcement is the threat of a punisher. It has the effect of
increasing the likelihood of the person repeating any action that allows him
to evade the punisher. In our scenario the possibility of another confrontation
in public with Dick is a negative reinforcer. It has the effect of increasing the
likelihood of Tom wearing a hard hat on Dick's shift in future. So a punisher
always reduces the likelihood of an action that is not wanted, and a negative
reinforcer always increases the likelihood of an alternative action that is more
desirable.

Recency effects

Not only did Dick remark on Tom not wearing a hat, he had him go off the
site to get one before he could go on with the job. By requiring Tom to actually reverse his actions that morning and come back onto the site wearing a
hat, Dick was using Guthrie's principle of recency — doing what you last did
— for breaking a bad habit and replacing it with a more suitable new one.
You may have noticed how particular actions of your own — like having a
swim after work on a Friday evening or lighting up a cigarette after a meal —
are associated (or conditioned in psychological terms) to events, times or
situations. This means that a situation is a *cue* or a *conditioned stimulus* for
you to respond in a certain way. In any given situation, we are most likely to
repeat what we last did when we were in that situation. Of course, this means
that the conditioned link between the situation and our response to it grows
stronger all the time, so that we become even more likely to repeat what we
last did in the situation as time goes on. This applies to our construction site
scenario in the following way: going onto the site has not become linked to
wearing a hat in Tom's case. Since *not* wearing a hat is what he last did when
going on site, he is likely to continue this unless this pattern of association is
broken and a new association which *does* link wearing a hat to going on site

is put in its place. By requiring Tom to go off the site and come back onto it wearing his hat, Dick is breaking the old link and beginning to build up a new one. On the Monday in question, wearing a hat became part of "doing what you last did" for Tom as far as his coming onto the site is concerned. Of course it is going to take a lot more than one single experience to build up a strong new habit of wearing a hat as a matter of course when coming onto a site. But at least Dick has started the ball rolling in the right direction from the safety point of view. This brings us to the next very important principle of behaviour that has to do with consistency and how consequences are scheduled to follow behaviour.

Consistency and consequences

If consequences are *certain* to follow an action, and if they happen quite soon after the action has taken place, they exert a much stronger influence over the behaviour than if they only sometimes follow it or do so after a delay. Dick remarked on the fact that Tom was not wearing a hat as soon as he noticed it and he *immediately* sent Tom to get a hat. So the consequences of Tom's behaviour followed his action without much delay. Further, we can gather from Bill saying "You should know your man by now" that Dick is very consistent in requiring the members of his shift to follow safety regulations. Dick's behaviour in this regard contrasts with that of Harry, the other foreman. Harry may or may not comment if someone isn't wearing a hat and he never sends someone off site immediately to get one. Consequently the members of his shift (including Tom) have a casual attitude towards safety.

Expenditure of effort

Nobody likes to expend effort. Much of our unsafe behaviour is due to this fact. The following examples of the kinds of things people will do to avoid expending effort will be quite familiar:

- Joe shins down a scaffold standard because he doesn't want the effort of walking to the end of the deck where there is a properly secured ladder

- Maura vents a tank in the laboratory while not wearing the regulation PPE. She doesn't want the effort of climbing the flight of stairs to the next floor to the PPE store

- Eileen carries a load of files and documents that is too heavy and awkwardly balanced because she doesn't want the extra effort involved in making two trips to the conference room

- Sean, an experienced electrician, decides to risk receiving a serious electric shock when installing a cable into an electrical panel without first isolating the panel. The means of isolating the panel is located a considerable distance away. Sean doesn't want the effort of going over there for a job that would only take him a short time.

In each of these examples, taking the risky option requires less effort than behaving safely. In our building site scenario, when Dick required Tom to go all the way back to the hut for a hat, he was reversing this balance and making it more of an effort for Tom to behave unsafely. Because Dick consistently insisted on the safety regulation being met immediately, it obviously takes less effort for Tom to wear a hat onto the site. If he doesn't, he is going to have to make two trips when one would do.

The moral of this principle of behaviour for supervisors, managers and systems and equipment designers who want to promote safety is to engineer systems and work settings so that unsafe actions require the person to expend *more* energy than do safe actions. In other words, they must make behaving dangerously cost more in terms of effort. We will have more to say on this point in Chapter 6 when we look at designing equipment for human use. For now the important thing to note and remember is that if behaving unsafely requires less effort than behaving safely, then people will take a risk. The supervisor/manager must intervene along lines similar to Dick's to make following safety regulations the more economic option.

Imitation effects

Learning by observing the behaviour of other people and the consequences which follow their behaviour is one of the most important kinds of learning people can do. Observing in this sense does not mean that we have to be physically present to witness the event. We can, and of course do, learn an enormous amount by reading about something that has happened to another person, or by watching what happens at one remove on TV or video. The people we observe in real life or via the media are models for us of how to act and react in a variety of situations which we may meet at some time or another ourselves. By imitating their behaviour we cut out the risks involved in learning by trial and error, and we also cut down on the time we would otherwise need to become competent members of society if we had to learn everything at first hand. The following are some examples of real life *vicarious learning* — that is, learning at one remove from the experience of others:

- a five year old girl observes a parent stopping at a busy road, looking right, left and right again, and waiting until the way is clear before stepping out. Because adults, and especially parents, are powerful and competent beings in a child's eyes, this little girl models her own behaviour on her parent's when she wants to cross a road in future. This means that she can avoid the danger of an accident which trail and error learning would involve

- Bob is new to the firm. The induction programme and staff handbook are useful in cueing him into the formal aspects of the organisation. He learns most about how the company *really* runs, though, by observing who emerge as the key players and how they behave. By modelling his own behaviour on that of successful co-workers, he quickly adapts his behaviour and attitudes to the company's culture.

In our construction site story we note that Mick learns what *not* to do by observing the consequences for Tom of not wearing a hat. Supervisors, managers and co-workers are all potential role models. An individual becomes a role model for any of a number of reasons. For example, someone who has the formal leadership position which goes with being a foreman, supervisor or manager may become a role model for the employees who work for them simply because of the power or influence they have in that role. A person who has acquired a status within a trade or profession because of his or her expertise may become a role model for younger, less experienced workers or even for his or her contemporaries. For instance, in our scenario there was a possibility that Tom would have become a negative role model for Mick if Dick had not intervened as he did. Tom was considered to be an expert in his area. As an apprentice, Mick would have been likely to model his behaviour on Tom's.

In psychological terms, "do what I say, not what I do" makes no sense at all. People — adults as well as children — learn by observation in most social situations, whether at home, school, work or leisure. Bad examples set by managers, supervisors and colleagues *will* be imitated whether we like it or not. The only solution is to ensure that the example given is always good. In this case, this means always being a model of safe behaviour.

Discrimination learning and the stimulus control of behaviour

Mention was made earlier of the fact that Tom and his colleagues were much more casual about safety when Harry was the shift foreman since he only expressed concern about hard hats and other safety matters intermittently. The difference in safety conscious behaviour shown by the workforce between Tom's shift and Harry's is an example of *discrimination learning* and the *stimulus control of behaviour*. Each foreman was a stimulus for different behaviour as regards safety. When Dick was on duty his presence was the stimulus for wearing hard hats and, we can assume, for attending to other safety matters on the site also. Harry's presence signalled an environment where poor safety performance would probably not be punished, or where if it was, the punishment would be very mild. The message here for promoting safer working is that while individual managers and supervisors (like Dick) can have an influence and can improve the safety situation through their own initiative, overall performance on safety will only improve if *all* members of an organisation are consistent in insisting that safety regulations are followed.

Positive reinforcement

Over time Dick notes that Tom regularly wears a hard hat on the site. He comments positively on this in terms that are personally important to Tom. (Tom is conscious of his position as a highly skilled member of his trade for which he is respected.) This *positive reinforcement* of Tom's safety conscious behaviour strengthens his tendency to work more safely, while the negative reinforcement of the possibility of another embarrassing confrontation with Dick weakens it. This combination of positive reinforcement of the desired course of action with negative reinforcement of the undesired behaviour is psychologically the most powerful pattern for maintaining safe behaviour over time. Positive reinforcement given in terms which are meaningful and acceptable to the recipient produces goodwill and a positive feeling about the situation. The person knows what action is required and what the consequences of not meeting that requirement will be. At the same time, he knows that meeting the requirement by acting in a particular way is noted and responded to positively.

A word of caution is in order before we leave this point. Positive reinforcement must be *genuine* if it is to be effective. This means that its use in the first place must arise out of a genuine commitment to, in this case, safety by the manager/supervisor. The form positive reinforcement takes must always be tailored to the values of the person receiving it. Only if it has personal meaning will it act as a positive reinforcement in the sense defined by Skinner — i.e. have the effect of making the behaviour which it follows more likely to be repeated. This means that supervisors and managers must know their employees well as individuals. A mechanical approach to reinforcement involving "off the shelf" schemes such as "the safest employee on site" etc. will not work in the long run and may alienate more people than they motivate if employees believe that it is not grounded in a genuine commitment to safety.

Extinction

Our story ends with Mick's move to another site where safety is not an issue one way or the other. The supervisors there neither punish failure to behave safely nor reinforce the following of safety regulations. In this situation, the good habits which Mick had learned on Dick's site gradually weaken until they stop altogether. *Extinction* is the technical term for this process of unlearning. Extinction occurs when behaviour is no longer reinforced. In many cases the dropping of an action or set of actions from a person's repertoire or stock of behaviours may not matter. In the case of safety, where not acting in accordance with regulations means that, by default, one is behaving in an unsafe way, it is critical that safe behaviour is consistently positively reinforced.

TO RECAP

The message of this chapter is that safe — or unsafe — work practices are learned. Because negative consequences so seldom follow risky behaviour, it is necessary for managers to engineer the workplace so that consequences *do* follow failure to follow safety regulations.

The process of engineering such consequences follows the *principles of learning* which have been researched and described in detail by such well-known psychologists as Pavlov, Skinner, Guthrie and Bandura. From the point of view of promoting safe working practices, the main principles of learning which managers and supervisors should apply are:

1. Making it clear that negative or punishing consequences follow risk taking and ensuring that such consequences are meaningful to the person concerned.

2. Ensuring that such consequences always follow the unsafe behaviour and do so immediately the behaviour is noticed.

3. Being aware of the power of example in promoting safe behaviour. This means that managers and supervisors must consistently be role models for working safely. People will do what you *do* — not what you say.

4. Being aware that people are essentially effort conserving. Usually behaving carelessly as regards safety takes less energy than behaving safely. Managers, supervisors and other professionals involved in promoting safety must design or redesign workplaces and equipment to reverse this state of affairs so that behaving safely becomes the easy (less effortful) option.

5. Just as unsafe behaviour must consistently be weakened by negative reinforcement (so that the person behaves safely to avoid punishment), working safely must be consistently strengthened by being positively reinforced. This means that supervisors and managers must be as alert and responsive to incidents of safe working as they are to examples of risk taking. They also need to know what matters to the individual employee so that they can promote safety through positive reinforcement that is meaningful to the person concerned.

6. Not reinforcing safe behaviour can lead to that behaviour being weakened and eventually dropping out of an employee's stock of behaviours altogether. Since not behaving safely means that by default one is behaving unsafely, managers and supervisors need to be consistently proactive in operating the principles of behaviour discussed in this chapter to promote safe working.

Chapter 4

Safety and the Individual — Accident Proneness

So far discussion has focused on issues related to safety policy. We began by considering the consequences for safety promotion of different policies on accident definition and recording. In the last chapter we looked at how people learn and noted how managerial policy and practice when responding to instances of unsafe behaviour by employees can promote safer working habits. In this chapter, and the next, the focus shifts to the individual and safety. Three distinct but related topics are considered. They are:

- accident proneness

- risk perception and risk taking

- the individual's understanding of and attitude towards safety at work.

The first of these — the complex issue of accident proneness — is examined in this chapter.

ACCIDENT PRONENESS

The idea of *accident proneness* springs readily to mind for many people when safety at work is being discussed. Most gatherings of safety personnel produce at least a couple of stories of the 'Jonahs' who seem to be dogged by misfortune and are repeatedly involved in mishaps of varying degrees of seriousness.

Traditionally, all definitions of accident proneness have at their core the notion of an inherent and permanent tendency to be involved in accidents. Farmer and Chambers[1] define accident proneness as "a personal idiosyncrasy of relative permanence predisposing the individual to a higher rate of accidents". According to Shaw and Sichel,[2] accident proneness "implies that

---

[1] Farmer, E. and Chambers, E.G. (1929) 'A Study of Personal Qualities in Accident Proneness and Proficiency', *Industrial Health Research Board*. London. Report No. 55.

[2] Shaw, L. S. and Sichel, H. S. (1971) *Accident Proneness*. Oxford: Pergamon.

even where exposed to the same conditions, some people are more likely to have accidents than others, or that people differ fundamentally in their innate propensity for accidents".

The idea of accident proneness holds appeal for many people as a way of explaining away accident repetition, so that neither the organisation nor the individual involved in the accidents has to find ways to improve the situation and/or performance on the job. However, recent research shows that it is more productive to look at the *process of accident involvement* than to simply (and fatalistically) categorise someone as accident prone on the basis of their safety history. The research findings that have led to this change of mind about the nature of accident proneness are considered next.

CRITIQUE OF RESEARCH ON ACCIDENT PRONENESS

The original data from which the concept of accident proneness was derived has been shown to be flawed and inadequate on a number of grounds. The notion of accident proneness was developed by Greenwood and Woods[3] to account for the statistical observation that the distribution of accidents in a population is not random. A random distribution would mean that each person in the population had an equal chance of being involved in an accident. This would be expected if accident involvement was a matter of chance alone. Instead, the distribution of accidents tends to cluster in a way that suggests that some people are more likely to be involved in accidents than are others. This *statistical* variation between individuals in numbers of accidents was called, by a psychological type term, "accident proneness" and, as Haight[4] notes, "the very suggestive name chosen for the variable parameter led many investigators to make a far more radical assumption; that every individual possesses a relatively constant value of λ, produced by his [*sic*] particular psycho-physical make-up".

In short, accident proneness came to be seen as an innate and unvarying characteristic of the person, rather like the colour of their eyes. The first flaw in Greenwood and Woods' work was to use a term with psychological connotations to explain what was simply a statistical observation. They did not attempt to consider the various alternative explanations that might have accounted for the distribution of accidents that they observed.

For example, Boyle[5] pointed out that researchers of accident proneness

---

[3] Greenwood, M. and Woods, H. M. (1919) 'The Incidence of Industrial Accidents upon Individuals with Special Reference to Multiple Accidents', *Industrial Fatigue Research Board*. London. Report No. 4.

[4] Haight, F. A. (1964) 'Accident Proneness, the History of an Idea', *Automobilismo E Automobilismo Industrial*. 12, pp. 534–46.

[5] Boyle, A. J. (1980) '"Found Experiments" in Accident Research: Report of a Study

need to take account of factors such as:

- how an accident is defined across studies

- how complete the reporting and recording of accidents and accident details are

- whether job centred and ambient (e.g. working conditions) risk factors are equal

- whether duration of exposure of employees to the risk is equal across studies

- how the statistical analysis is carried out.

Greenwood and Woods did not control for these factors, and Boyle notes that many researchers who followed in their footsteps did not do so either.

The findings of research studies that *did* take account of alternative explanations for the non-random distribution of accidents between people show that:

- the non-random distribution of accidents (known as the negative binomial distribution) on which Greenwood and Woods based the concept could be due to differences between jobs in the level of risk involved.[6] Thus, what appeared to be a feature of the individual may actually have been a feature of the job he or she was doing

- the binomial distribution could also be obtained if the occurrence of an accident alters the probability of having further accidents in the future.[7] This state of affairs could come about if people began to think of themselves as accident prone, having been involved in one accident. It may also lead to others thinking of them in this way. As a result, their performance might become clumsy through over-monitoring their actions. You may have experienced the last point yourself when you were at the early stages of learning a new skill, like golf for example. Over-monitoring also leads to the breakdown of well established skills, like car driving or typing. Try becoming conscious of the motion of letting the clutch out or of how pre-

---

of Accident Rates and Implications for Future Research', *Journal of Occupational Psychology*. 53, (1), pp. 53–64.

[6] Arbous, A.G. and Kerrich, J. E. (1951) 'Accident Statistics and the Concept of Accident Proneness', *Biometrics*. 7, (4), pp. 340–42. See also Irwin, J. O. (1964) 'Comments on the paper: Chambers, E. C and Yule, G. U., "Theory and Observation in the Investigation of Accident Causation"', *Journal of the Royal statistical Society (Supplement)*, 7, pp. 89–109.

[7] McKenna, F. P. (1983) 'Accident Proneness: A Conceptual Analysis', *Accident Analysis and Prevention*. 15, (1), 65–71.

cisely you strike individual keys on your keyboard. You will find that you'll stall the engine and your typing will go completely haywire. The same principle operates when someone who has had one accident becomes over-conscious of their performance when they are next in the accident setting. Their performance can become clumsy or break down completely. Their actions may also become indecisive through worry that they will have another accident. They may dither about beginning to feed a machine or pulling out at a crossroads. Other people too may contribute to their clumsiness or anxiety by urging them to "be careful this time" and so on. This sets up a psychologically vicious circle of anxiety leading to clumsiness or indecisiveness, which may indeed result in an accident or near miss. This in turn increases the anxiety and clumsiness. The overall end result may be the "self-fulfilling prophecy".[8] This is the state of affairs where the person's belief that they are accident prone is confirmed and strengthened by their being involved in more accidents because of the operation of the vicious circle of preoccupation, leading to poor performance, leading to further preoccupation

- people are not consistently equally accident prone across all situations, which should be the case if accident proneness were a trait in the traditional sense in which the construct was originally used.[9] So, a person may have accidents at home *or* at work *or* at leisure *or* across some combination of these locations, but rarely, if ever, in *all* of them. She may have accidents when driving but not when cycling, or when cooking but not when house cleaning, or when on the sports field but not in the gym. If accident involvement itself involved the kind of trait-like construct which accident proneness is traditionally defined as being, this situation-specific pattern of accidents should not be found

- people are not consistently accident prone. Hansen[10] points out that research shows that people rarely if ever regularly have repeated accidents throughout the *whole* of their life span (i.e. from infancy through childhood, teenage years and adulthood into old age)

- when psychological tests of personality are used to identify accident proneness, a number of traits, some unrelated to each other, have been associ-

---

[8] Corey, M. (1988) 'Delta Airline's Problems as a Function of Self-Fulfilling Prophecy', *Psychology: A Journal of Human Behaviour.* 25, (2), pp. 59–63.

[9] Adelstein, A. M. (1952) 'Accident Proneness: A Criticism of the Concept Based Upon an Analysis of Shunter's Accidents', *Journal of the Royal Statistical Society.* Series A, 115, pp. 354–410.

[10] Hansen, C. P. (1988) 'Personality Characteristics of the Accident Involved Employee', *Journal of Business and Psychology.* 2, (4), pp. 346–5.

ated with accident involvement from time to time. Thus accident proneness does not appear to be a single, clear-cut psychometric entity[11]

- more generally, within the last twenty-five years or so, the traditional trait approach to individual differences has been critically reviewed by psychologists and has been replaced by a more process focused 'state' view of personality. This change of emphasis in psychological theory is obviously of major importance for our understanding of individual differences in accident involvement, so we will look at it in more detail in the next section.

THE TRAIT CONSTRUCT AND ACCIDENT PRONENESS

We can define a trait as "an underlying attribute that is characteristic of a person throughout their life time and across situations". Looking back to the definitions of accident proneness given earlier in this chapter by Farmer and Chambers and Shaw and Sichel, it is clear that these researchers understood accident proneness in this traditional sense. Since the mid-1960s, the concept of a trait as a basically permanent and fixed element of personality has been gradually discarded within psychology because the research evidence does not support it.

Traits were first proposed by psychologists to account for the consistencies of people's behaviour over time and across situations.[12] However, as researchers observed more and more people across a wider range of settings, they noted that people did *not* always exhibit the same pattern of behaviour, but instead adapted their actions and their style to meet the needs of particular circumstances. Research from developmental psychologists showed that people also changed their behaviour over time. A shy schoolchild could become a relaxed and confident adult through a combination of acquiring social skills and growing in self-confidence as he successfully dealt with different experiences. In the face of this evidence, the trait construct came to be discarded. Summarising the position in the 1980s, Mischel[13] wrote that "highly generalised behavioural consistencies have not been demonstrated, and the concept of personality traits as broad response dispositions is thus untenable".

The consistencies which we see in our own and each other's behaviour results from the fact that we usually encounter those others in a limited set of more or less similar (if not actually identical) circumstances. For example, we meet people in work settings or in social or leisure settings and, depend-

[11]Haddon, W., Suchman, E. A. and Klein, D. (Eds.) (1964) *Accident Proneness*. New York: Harper & Row.

[12]Allport, G.W. (1937) *Personality: A Psychological Interpretation*. New York: Holt.

[13]Mischel, W. (1986) *Introduction to Personality*. 4th ed. New York: Holt, Rinehart & Winston.

ing upon our degree of friendship with them, at home in more or less formal circumstances. The consistency lies in the interaction between the individual and the setting which calls forth the same behaviour pattern over and over (and will continue to do so as long as the behaviour works to the individual's satisfaction). Thus consistency of behaviour does not depend upon some predetermined, fixed personality trait within the person.

The message for those concerned with accident prevention and accident research is clear. Instead of looking for the key to an individual's involvement in accidents in his or her personality, we need to look at the situation in which the accidents occur to discover what *combinations* of features of the individual's task relevant psychology (knowledge, abilities, skills and other characteristics) and the work setting is giving rise to the accident. In the case where a person goes through a period when she is involved in a number of accidents, it may be found that she is experiencing a higher than usual degree of stress at work, at home or in other areas of life involving personal relationships.

THE PUZZLE OF DIFFERENTIAL ACCIDENT INVOLVEMENT

So far in this chapter we have seen that there is no evidence for a concept of accident proneness as a unitary, fixed and unvarying feature of a person's psychology, which *causes* someone to have accidents repeatedly throughout life and across the full range of situations encountered. On the other hand, inequality in likelihood of accident involvement of certain categories of people is widely recognised. For example, insurance companies charge high premiums to young car drivers, and to young male drivers in particular. There is also research data that show that while an individual may not be accident prone in the traditional sense, he may have more accidents than would be expected by chance at some stage of his life or in some circumstance. For example, Boyle reports a correlation of 0.69 between the number of accidents involving injury for the same individuals across the two halves of a period of eight years and nine months. If accident proneness is not a viable construct, how can we account for this evidence of accident repetition?

FROM ACCIDENT PRONENESS TO UNDERSTANDING THE DYNAMICS OF ACCIDENT INVOLVEMENT

The alternative position to the accident proneness view focuses on the dynamics of how people come to be repeatedly involved in accidents at particular periods in their lives. It examines the psychological processes of information processing and of socialisation in the workplace and in society as a whole, which create a situation from which accident repetition can arise.

The essence of this approach to repeated accident involvement is that accident repetition comes about because of the way in which the person is approaching, dealing with and/or reacting to the task on hand and/or her life situation at the time. The person's life situation can include the setting in which the job is being done, the organisation's climate and culture as perceived by the person, and the person's situation at home and in her personal life.

Issues like the person's age, degree of self-confidence and personal security or insecurity, emotional maturity and susceptibility to peer or group pressure are all relevant in the accident repetition approach. Of particular importance to this approach is the view that while there will always be a section of the population who possess the age and psychological characteristics which are associated with having repeated accidents, the membership of this group changes over time.[14] As people grow older and become wiser, more self-confident, less insecure and less in need of the approval of others, they move out of the group of potential accident repeaters, leaving others to take their place until they too mature and move out.

From this perspective, strategies to remedy repeated involvement in accidents would focus on examining the safety climate of the organisation and how this is perceived by the accident involved person, as well as by the staff in general. The person's performance in the real life work situation is examined in order to identify any ergonomic factors that might be contributing to the accident. Training and retraining, giving particular attention to error analysis, are important. It is also important to take into account any stresses that the person may be experiencing on the job, at work or at home, bearing in mind that some of these may be related to the personal style of the accident repeaters as discussed in the next section of this chapter.

The accident repetition approach evidently contrasts with that of accident proneness in a quite major way. Accident repetition is a *temporary* state of the accident involved person over a particular period of time, due to some physical or psychological mismatch between the person and the task or work situation. This mismatch is essentially modifiable. On the other hand, the essence of accident proneness is that it is a *fixed* and immutable personality trait. As such the accident repetition approach reflects a more positive attitude to workplace safety generally, and a more proactive approach to safety management.

Let us now look at the evidence for the temporary state view of repeated accident involvement.

---

[14]Hansen, C. P. (1989) 'A Causal Model of the Relationship among Accidents, Biodata, Personality and Cognitive Factors', *Journal of Applied Psychology*. 74, (1), pp. 81–90.

Evidence for Accident Repetition as a Temporary State

The relevant research data are of two kinds. First there is research on the *personal style* of accident repeaters versus non-repeaters. Personal style refers to the way in which a person relates to others and thinks about the world and his place in it. For example, one person may be generally less talkative and less outgoing than another in social situations. Using psychological terms, we would say that this person was more introverted than extroverted. People may also differ from each other on whether they approach life with a generally positive, optimistic attitude or whether they generally expect the worst. Personal style can be changed if circumstances and personal choice require it. Our introvert will be able to be more outgoing and extroverted if that is required by circumstances. Personal style is one's *preferred* way of relating to the world at a given point of time, but it does not in any way mean that one cannot act differently.[15] Personal style also changes with time and experience. Dealing specifically with the question of personal style and safety, Hansen[16] notes:

> The old accident proneness theory did not allow for the fact that people change over time. Thus, a person could be quite immature at age 22, but later have experiences causing him to 'grow up' by age 26. His accident rate at age 22 would, therefore, not correlate with his rate four years later because he is no longer the same type of person.

The second type of research data relates to differences between accident repeaters and non-repeaters in the way in which they process task relevant information. As we shall see, there is evidence that people differ in how easily they are distracted by aspects of the task or workplace that are not relevant to the task on hand. Because we have limited information processing capacity, mistakes can be made if some of that capacity is diverted towards irrelevant issues and away from the main task or its main aspect. This point will be discussed more fully in a later section of this chapter. For now we need only note that being easily distracted may be a critical factor in the susceptibility of a person to an accident in certain kinds of work situations.

---

[15]The fact that one can change does not mean that this may not sometimes be difficult to do, of course. Personal style is one's habitual way of relating to the world and, like any habit, it will take time, real commitment and much effort to change. Professional advice from a psychologist may be useful.

[16]Hansen, C. P. (1988) *op cit.*

Personal Style Differences between Accident Repeaters and Non-Repeaters

Researchers have identified four aspects of personal style which differentiate accident repeaters from non-repeaters. They are:

1. An external locus of control with regard to safety and safety related matters.[17]

2. A low level of awareness of the interpersonal and performance aspects of behaviour relevant to working safely.[18]

3. A tendency to be physically tense, anxious and low in self-confidence.[19]

4. A tendency[20] to be high on extroversion.[21]

Let us now look at these aspects of personal style in a little more detail, noting how each relates to the psychology of working safely.

Locus of control refers to whether or not we see ourselves as being able to take action to influence our situation. People with an *external* locus of control generally consider themselves to be at the mercy of circumstances, chance or the whim of other people. They believe others are more influential or powerful than they. As a result they are unlikely to take action to correct a situation which has 'gone against' them. If they do take action, they are less likely to persist if at first they don't succeed. In contrast, those with an *internal* locus of control will take action in most situations since their belief is that there is always something they can do to influence a situation in their favour.

---

[17]Jones, J. W. and Wuebeker, L. (1985) 'Development and Validation of the Safety Locus of Control Scale', *Perceptual and Motor Skills.* 61, pp. 151–61.

[18]Hansen, C. P. (1988) *op cit.*

[19]*Ibid.*

[20]*Ibid.*

[21]The research linking high scores on extroversion to accident repetition holds only in American and Western European societies. Researchers in India have found that high extroversion is associated with less accident repetition (Kunda, S.R (1957) 'A Psychological Study of Accidents in a Factory', *Educational Psychology*, 4, pp. 17–28; Pestonjee, D. M. and Singh, U. B. (1980) 'Neuroticism – Extroversion as Correlates of Accident Occurrence', *Accident Analysis and Prevention*, 12, pp. 201–4). The reason for this cross-cultural difference is that extroversion has two components — *sociability* and *sensation seeking*. It is likely that those who took part in the Western and US research scored high on extroversion by scoring high on sensation seeking, while their Indian counterparts' extroversion score was made up mainly of high scores on the sociability component. The Indian focus on sociability may give rise to greater awareness of and concern for the impact of one's own behaviour on colleagues. Sensation seeking by its nature is more self-focused and is less likely to result in concern for others.

Applied to safety, locus of control refers to whether people see themselves as being able to improve the safety level of their job or workplace. People with an external locus of control about safety are inclined to hold the view that accidents just happen but that if anything *can* be done, only management can do it. Those with an internal safety locus of control believe that they can influence safety levels. Consequently they are more likely to take action to improve their chances of staying safe on the job. Examples of proactive safety behaviour from a person with an internal locus of control might be:

- wearing personal protection equipment

- attending safety courses

- being watchful for hazards and reporting them

- being careful not to create hazards by failing to follow safety rules and guidelines on matters like housekeeping and the safe operation of equipment.

A number of studies in settings including hotels, hospitals, chemical companies, bus companies, a trucking firm and a milk delivery company have all found that people with an external locus of control for safety were more likely to be involved in accidents than those with an internal locus.[22] Furthermore, the *severity* of the accident also seems to be related to locus of control. People with a more external locus tend to have more serious accidents.[23]

One of the most consistent research findings distinguishing *some* accident repeaters from non-repeaters has been the evidence for low social awareness and poor performance on aspects of behaviour relevant to working safely. By comparison with people who were not repeatedly involved in accidents, those who were so involved had certain characteristics:

- they rated high on impulsive, carefree and adventurous behaviour

- they were more easy going and indifferent to the rights of others

- they were more inclined to be hostile and uncooperative, especially towards authority

- they tended to 'act out' emotionally by becoming verbally (and sometimes physically) abusive under pressure

- they were more likely to engage in horseplay, behave in macho ways and

---

[22]Wuebeker, L. J. (1986) 'Safety Locus of Control as a Predictor of Industrial Accidents and Injuries', *Journal of Business and Psychology.* 1, (1), pp. 19–30.

[23]Wuebeker, L. J., Jones, J. W. and Dubois, D. (1985) 'Safety Locus of Control and Employee Accidents', *Technical Report: The St Paul Companies.* St Paul MN.

take unnecessary risks to prove a point or to keep up appearances before their peers.

This *low socialisation accident repeater profile* appears to be one of two profiles associated with accident repetition. The second profile found for repeaters is not so clear-cut.[24] However, the indications are that *some* people who have repeated accidents are particularly high on anxiety, physical tension and worry. They tend to be indecisive. They may feel nervous, be easily fatigued and be particularly sensitive to criticism (or feedback which they see as criticism). There is also some evidence that accident repeaters of this kind may be self-critical and may easily become depressed.[25] This profile is more or less a mirror image of the low socialisation one. It is likely that the person susceptible to the self-fulfilling prophecy dynamic discussed earlier will come from this category of accident repeater.

Scoring high on extroversion means that the person concerned is sociable and outgoing, likes stimulation and excitement and is less inclined to enjoy his or her own company or quieter, more contemplative activities. Hansen[26] says: "the introverted person is described as quiet, intellectual, organised and emotionally controlled. In contrast, the extrovert is sociable, lively, novelty-seeking, carefree and emotionally expressive". So, as you see there are many links between extreme extroversion and the low socialisation profile described earlier. In my opinion, it is not useful to use extroversion alone as an indicator of likelihood of accident repetition. This is because as it relates to accident repetition, high extroversion is just one element in a complex matrix of factors that create the potential for accident repetition. High extroversion on its own (without the other elements of the low socialisation profile) need have no association with accident repetition. The low socialisation profile, of which high extroversion is a part, gives more relevant information on personal style in this area.

INFORMATION PROCESSING DIFFERENCES BETWEEN ACCIDENT REPEATERS AND NON-REPEATERS

Accident repeaters and non-repeaters differ on distractibility.[27] As well as

---

[24]Hansen, C. P. (1988) *op cit.*
[25]Craske, S. (1968) 'A Study of the Relation between Personality and Accident History', *British Journal of Medical Psychology*. 41, pp. 399–404.
[26]Hansen, C. P. *op cit.*
[27]Hanson, C. P (1989) *op cit*: Porter, C. S. (1988) 'Accident Proneness: A Review of the Concept', *International Review of Ergonomics*. 2, pp. 177–206; Houghton, née Porter, C. S. and Corlett, E. N. (1989) 'Performance Differences of Individuals Classified by Questionnaire as Accident Prone or Non-Accident Prone', *Ergonomics*. 32, (3), pp. 317–33.

knowing what a particular job requires and having the skills to do it, efficient, effective and safe working often requires that the person has the ability to maintain a level of attention appropriate to the nature of the task sometimes for quite long periods of time. (A task which is new and/or complex will require a greater level of attention than a well practised task which is relatively straightforward.)

Distractibility refers to the ease with which a person's attention may be diverted from the task on hand by some other aspect of the workplace or by her own thoughts and feelings. Hansen found that people's self-assessment of how distractible they were was related to repeated accident involvement. In a study of the actual performance of accident involved and non-accident involved people on a task designed to test their distractibility, Porter-Houghton and Corlett found significant differences between the two groups. In this study participants had to perform two tasks at once. The main task was to return as many tennis balls as possible in a fifteen second interval in a computerised game. The secondary task (which made it a dual task situation), was a "blind reach" one in which the participants had to leave a mark at the centre of a target hidden from them by a screen. The location of the target was signalled by different tones. For example, a high pitched, loud tone played intermittently meant that the target was placed behind the bottom right vertical part of the screen. A low pitched, quiet, continuous tone meant it was in the horizontal top left area. The participants had to attempt to pinpoint the target's centre by leaving a mark on the screen at the point where they thought the centre was. Participants were told that the ball batting task was the main one and that they should keep that going no matter what. They should try to do their best on the secondary target location task.

The psychological situation created was one of high cognitive or information processing load. The participants had to maintain a high level of attentiveness throughout the forty-five minute test period if they were to do well on either or both tasks. Results showed that high scorers on the researchers' accident proneness scale[28] did less well on the ball batting task in terms of numbers of balls returned. They were slower than the low scorers on the target location task. The researchers claimed that the performance deficits exhibited by the high accident proneness participants arose because they had more difficulties in coping with the distracting effects of the tasks on each other. The participants who rated themselves as low on accident proneness did better because they were better able to divide their attention between the two tasks and to resist the distracting effects of the target task when they were working on the ball batting, and vice versa.

---

[28] Although they agree that "accident proneness" is a confusing term, the researchers use it because their report was written before the new terms "repeater" and "differential accident involvement" had come into vogue.

In the ordinary course of events there is obviously ample opportunity for dual task situations to arise at work. Other people are working nearby. People are coming and going, and phone calls and conversations are taking place in the immediate vicinity. Aspects of production or administrative processes may vary unusually and emergencies may arise. Some or all of these have the potential to grab the attention of the person. (Attention is 'grabbed' by new, infrequent, novel or personally important events. This issue will be discussed further in the next chapter.)

Sources of distraction can also come from within the person. If someone has serious concerns about their health, personal life or family, they are likely to find their mind drifting off job related issues to thinking and worrying about these matters.

The research just outlined shows that individuals differ in their capacity to resist distractions, whatever the source. Where a task requires concentrated and sustained attention, the person who has difficulty in resisting the distracting effects of happenings or thoughts and feelings not relevant to the task is potentially more likely to be involved in accidents than is someone who is not so easily distracted.

POLICY AND MANAGEMENT APPLICATIONS

What use can policy makers and managers make of the information on accident repetition presented here? Steps that *can* be taken fall into immediate and longer-term categories of action.

An obvious immediate step, but one which may be overlooked, especially if the employer or manager believes in the traditional accident proneness view, is to re-examine incident and accident records and sites carefully. The aim of this is to ensure that ergonomic (machine design) and other situational factors which might have contributed to an accident have been corrected. There are cases where machines are not continuously preventatively maintained and where site housekeeping has been allowed to become casual. From what we know of the nature of accidents (refer back to Chapter 1), it will only be a matter of time before another incident occurs. If the same person is working at this task, she will obviously be the person involved in the event. Consequently it will look *as if* she is accident prone, although the fault will actually lie in the situation rather than the person.

The employer/manager can immediately assign potential accident repeaters to less hazardous tasks while longer-term strategies for promoting safety are put in place. It is important to bear in mind that repeated accident involvement is a state rather than a trait. As such it is amenable to modification over time and in circumstances which clearly make safety a priority. As we saw in Chapter 3, safety relevant attitudes and behaviours are learned through experience. Where the organisation has a strong safety culture, an employee will adapt his behaviour over time to fit with the prevailing values of the group. This means that, even where a new recruit to the workforce starts out with poor safety attitudes and behaviour, he can be expected to improve in the regard once he learns the culture of the organisation. At this point he may be assigned to more hazardous tasks if required.

Where a strong safety culture does not already exist, the first longer-term strategy is to put one in place. This is the only strategy with a real chance of significantly improving safety at work in general and in the specific case of the low socialisation, external locus of control accident repeater. If safety is consistently taken seriously by all levels of management, this will create a climate where peer and group influence will act in tandem with management policy and practice to quickly suppress the risky behaviour and 'macho' attitudes of this kind of accident involved employee. The processes of conditioning and social learning that can be used to create a safety culture were described in the last chapter.

The second kind of profile linked with accident repetition involves a tendency towards self-criticism, tension, a lack of self-confidence and excessive worry. People with this profile who are involved in accidents would probably benefit from retraining on the job that focuses on identifying and correcting the particular kinds of errors they make. General training will be of little use. The training must focus on the specific deficits in the employee's performance, which should be corrected on the spot. The employee should then be given the opportunity to *over learn* the corrected performance element.

Over learning is a training technique used to help stress-proof performance on tasks with serious consequences if an error occurs. It means that the skill is learned to *and beyond* the point where the learning curve levels out (known as the asymptote). Figure 4.1 illustrates this.

Figure 4.1: Over learning a skill

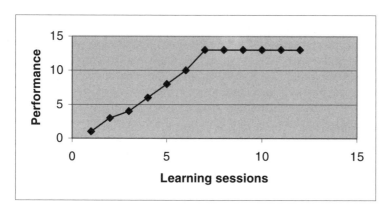

Examples of over learning can be found in literature on the training of military personnel. If an emergency arises, personnel trained in this way do not have to think twice about the action to take. They automatically swing into the appropriate response because they have been so thoroughly trained on the job.

The worry/anxiety aspect of the approach to their work of employees with this second type of accident repeater profile could be addressed using a psychological technique used by sports psychologists. Sports psychologists tutor athletes in positive self-talk which they can use to focus and motivate themselves during performance. We do this in our heads most of the time — it is rather like a running commentary on:

• what we see around us — "That's a funny looking hat"

• ourselves and our performance — "That was as neat a deal as I've seen, even if I say so myself" or "You made a right mess of that one, Murphy"

• other people — "What a clown!"

• situations and events.

Generally our self-talk is fairly innocuous and slips through our mind like clouds across a sky. Occasionally we latch on to one aspect of the commentary and begin to run it over and over again. Where this is negative in tone, and we can't readily stop it, we are worrying.

The self-talk of the accident involved worrier is likely to centre on fear of failure — "I'm bound to run into it again" or "I don't *really* understand this thing! I'm not in control". Using the self-talk technique, the person is guided by the psychologist to become more aware of negative and irrelevant thoughts and is shown how to replace them with more positive and task focused ones. This will help break the vicious circle which was discussed earlier in this chapter and which can result in a self-fulfilling prophecy as regards accidents.

Finally, you may be wondering why I haven't mentioned an obvious and simple application of the research on accident involvement — its use in the areas of personnel selection and deployment. Specifically you may be thinking of using the two profiles to identify applicants or employees with accident repeater potential and then to deselect these individuals. In fact, the low socialisation, external locus of control criteria was used to guide the hiring policy of a trucking firm and a milk delivery company. The trucking firm used the profile in the recruitment of new employees over a forty-one month period. The result was that monthly paid insurance losses were reduced from $25,000 in Phase A (the pre-profile recruitment period) to $5,400 in Phase B (the profile recruitment period). In the case of the milk delivery company, a downward trend in worker compensation accidents was noted over the two years subsequent to using the profile for personnel selection in comparison with the two preceding years. However, the researchers who did this study note that the results may not be as simple to interpret as they appear.

Jones and Wuebeker[29] note that changes in the organisation taking place when they did their research, but which were not formally part of their intervention, may have affected their results. They note that using psychometric tests that emphasised safety as part of the personnel selection procedure "would communicate to all employees that management is fully committed to improving workplace safety. *An improved organisational 'climate for safety' could evolve*" (my italics). In this statement, Jones and Wuebeker are suggesting that the employees adapted their behaviour to fit in with the new safety consciousness of the organisation's culture. Obviously if the characteristics involved in the low socialisation, external locus of control profile were traits in the traditional sense, the employees would not have been able to modify their behaviour in this way. The point is, of course, that any organisation with a strong safety culture will tend to elicit safer behaviour from its employees. This means that personnel selection and deployment procedures that emphasise accident liability at the time the selection or deployment decision is being made may be ignoring the longer-term potential gain to the organisation of the person's other skills, knowledge and abilities. Social and emotional maturity, self-confidence and independence from group and peer pressure develop with age and experience from most people.

Rather than not employing somebody with job relevant potential but who also has the potential for accident involvement (according to the psychometric profile), the manager/employer might be wiser to look at factors like creating a safety culture at work, attending to ergonomic aspects of the workplace, and emphasising on-the-job training which focuses on identifying and eliminating errors in performance.

Adopting these kinds of policies has advantages for both the employer and employee. The latter is not discriminated against on the basis of a temporary phase which is essentially modifiable, and which he or she is likely to outgrow or resolve with the minimum of assistance. The employer retains the person's task relevant skills and abilities in the organisation's human resource pool, ready to be drawn on at the appropriate time over the longer term.

[29]Jones, J. W. and Wuebeker, L. J. (1988) 'Accident Prevention Through Personnel Selection', *Journal of Business and Psychology*. 3, (2), pp. 187–98.

Chapter 5

The Individual and Safety — Perceiving and Taking Risks

WHY DID THEY DO IT?

A farmer attempted to clear a blockage on a large round baler. He did not shut off the power take-off mechanism and he did not switch off the tractor. He attempted to clear the blockage using his foot. He was drawn into the baler and he suffered fatal injuries.

A worker was badly injured when he fell twenty feet through corrugated asbestos cement roof sheeting. He was employed by a contractor who had been engaged to carry out repairs on the roofs of two buildings. The contractor supervised the work on the first building where crawling ladders were used and proper edge protection was provided. The contractor gave clear instructions that similar precautions should be taken in doing the second roof. The workers did not make proper use of the equipment provided. As a result, one man fell through the asbestos cement sheeting.

Discussion of incidents like these often takes a form that suggests that the person(s) involved in the event intentionally took a risk. We say things like "why didn't he use the guard?" or "didn't she know the hood would fall if the hinge was loose?". The implication is that the incident/accident could have been avoided if those involved had judged or acted more prudently.

There is general agreement among researchers that risk involves three elements.[1] These are:

1. The potential loss of something.

2. The significance of that loss to those affected should the loss occur.

3. The probability or likelihood of the loss actually occurring.

---

[1] Yates, J.F. and Stone, E.R (1992) 'The Risk Construct' In J. F Yates (Ed.) *Risk-taking Behaviour*. Chichester: Wiley & Sons.

I add a fourth element to this list. This is:

4.   The potential gain from the action should the loss not occur.

In the farming example above, the potential gain to the farmer would have been the effort and time saved in not turning off the power take-off mechanism and the tractor engine had he got away with the risk.

When we talk as if people intentionally take risks, we are assuming that they think in certain ways when facing danger. First, we assume that the people see or perceive the potential for loss which the situation entails. Second, we are assuming that they carry out an objective assessment of the loss involved should the situation go wrong. In doing this they may judge the loss to be insignificant in absolute terms or relative to the possible gains. They may judge the loss to be unlikely to occur. They may assess the situation as involving some combination of these factors which makes it seem worthwhile to take the risk. At all events, the implication is that people take *calculated risks*.

In this chapter we look at what studies of the psychology of taking risks tell us about the truth or otherwise of this assumption. More specifically, we will look at the features of a situation which leads us to perceive it as involving risk. We then consider the factors which influence our judgement of the riskiness of situations in general, and in particular where we ourselves are concerned. Finally, we look at the influence on risk taking of factors other than the probability that our actions will result in loss. Among these factors are issues like pressure from colleagues and the impact on earnings of *not* taking a risk.

THE PERCEPTION OF THE POTENTIAL FOR LOSS

When judging whether or not a situation is hazardous, we usually use two criteria. These are the degree of dread risk and of unknown risk which the situation involves.[2] *Dread risk* refers to how uncontrollable a situation is and how irreversible, catastrophic or fatal the consequences of the event are. It also involves a judgement about whether the person affected has or doesn't have a choice about engaging with the risk, and whether or not he or she could choose to escape from the risk once exposed to it. *Unknown risk* refers to the extent to which the hazard is observable and its effects are immediately obvious to those exposed. This aspect of risk also includes whether the hazard is an old and well known one so that its consequences are known to and understood by scientists, policy makers and others who might be expected to legislate for, and deal with, the situation.

---

[2] Slovic, P. (1987) 'Perception of Risk', *Science*. Vol. 236, April 17, pp. 280–85.

Table 5.1 gives examples of the kinds of questions which people are likely to ask themselves when making an assessment of the dangerousness of a situation or course of action.

Table 5.1: Questions asked when assessing the danger in a situation or course of action

Can I avoid the hazard if I wish — or do I have no choice in the matter?
If I have to face it, can I control how it affects me?
If something goes wrong, is the result catastrophic (i.e. disabling injury or death)?
If something goes wrong, can the risk be contained or reduced, or will the risk continue to increase?
If something goes wrong, will it affect my children in the future?
Are the effects observable? Will I know if something has gone wrong?
Do scientists and medical specialists know the risks involved in the situation?
Can scientists and medical specialists treat or deal with any negative results that may occur?

Figure 5.1 is extracted from the research report in which the factors of dread risk and unknown risk were identified. The quadrant labelled A is the low perceived risk space in the grid. Given the proportion of farm accidents which involve tractors (six in 1998 according to HSA figures), and the high rate of road traffic accidents in general (355 Irish road traffic deaths for the period 1 January–28 October 1999), it is interesting to see that tractors, motor vehicles, motor cycles and bicycles are all perceived as non-hazardous by the layperson.

Figure 5.1: The location of some common objects and activities in 'perceived risk' space

(based on Slovic, 1987)

THE SIGNIFICANCE OF THE LOSS

Table 5.2 is based on Green and Brown's study of the perceived seriousness of different kinds of losses resulting from accidents at work.[3] You will notice that two outcomes (paralysis from the neck down and brain damage) were judged by their respondents to be a loss worse than death itself.

Table 5.2: Rank order of perceived 'dreadfulness' of different injuries

Bruises
Sprained ankle
Concussion
Simple fracture of arm
Broken ribs
Compound fracture of arm
Internal injuries
Fractured skull
Carbon monoxide poisoning
Multiple facial lacerations
Loss of one eye
Loss of right arm
Severe burning over one third of body
Loss of one leg
Radiation sickness
Paralysis from waist down
Loss of sight of both eyes
Death
Paralysis from neck down
Brain damage

THE PROBABILITY OF THE LOSS OCCURRING

The final link in the chain of risk assessment concerns a person's judgement of how likely it is that the potential for loss will actually materialise. Of

[3] Green, C. H. and Brown, R. A (1978) *The Acceptability of Risk: Summary Report.* Boreham Wood: Fire Research Station.

particular interest to us here is a person's judgement of how likely its is that the potential for loss will be realised in his or her specific case. First we shall look at the factors which affect our ability to make judgements about probabilities in general. Then we shall focus on the factors that influence us when we are considering the likelihood that our own actions might result in loss to ourselves or those for whom we feel responsible.

Judging Probability in General

Probability is a statistical concept used to estimate the likelihood of a given event occurring. Statisticians and other professionals who use statistics in their work (e.g. insurance assessors and actuaries) estimate the chances of a given event occurring by chance alone. Then they examine the effect of different conditions, such as age, health, gender and occupation, on this estimate. Their aim is to identify those conditions that significantly influence the chances of a given outcome, making it more or less likely to occur than chance alone would indicate.

It is on the basis of this procedure that car insurers load the premiums of young male drivers. Statistical studies of car accidents show that the chances of young men being involved in an accident are significantly greater than chance alone would suggest. Contrariwise, but based on the same probability estimation procedure, women drivers are offered a more favourable deal, since car accident statistics show that on average they are less likely to be involved in an accident than chance would predict.

It is evident that the car insurer is taking a *calculated* risk in offering insurance cover to different types of drivers. Can it also be said that the man or woman in the street calculates risk in a similar way as they go about their daily life?

The answer to this question is *not usually*. Contrary to what many people believe, human decision making in the ordinary course of events is not an entirely logical process of reviewing, weighing and rationally balancing *all* the information available on an issue before coming to a decision based on the facts of the matter. Instead we base our judgement of the likely consequences of our action on quite imprecise rules which we devise on the basis of our experience, or on the impression which we have formed of the issue involved. These imprecise rules based on the impression we have of an issue, or on our limited personal experience of it, are called *heuristics*. As an example of a heuristic, let us look at the data on the risk to health which results from smoking.

Although medical research has documented a link between smoking and various kinds of heart and lung diseases, many people still smoke. They may justify the risk they take by referring to someone they know who "... smoked sixty cigarettes a day for years, was never sick and died at ninety-seven". This is an example of what is known as the *representativeness bias* heuristic.

We will look at this in more detail later in this chapter. For the moment, note that this heuristic does not in any way involve *calculating* the risk involved. The person does not gather and assess the facts of the matter in a mathematical and rational way. Instead he picks an example from his own experience and bases the probability of illness resulting from his risky behaviour on this very selective sample.

Because we usually use heuristics when judging probability in general, the judgement of statistical probabilities by laypeople is quite poor. People do not usually think in precise quantitative terms in these situations. (If they did, human behaviour would look very different from what it does — so much time would be spent referring to actuarial tables and carrying out complicated calculations of probable outcomes for this or that course of action, that we should have very little time for acting on the results of our risk assessment!) Indeed, even experts such as insurance assessors and medical researchers probably do not calculate the risks attached to their behaviour when off duty, but use heuristics like the rest of us.

Thinking about probabilities with the aid of heuristics can bias our judgement of the likelihood of given events in certain ways.[4] Studies of laypeople's probability estimates have consistently shown us to be prone to the following biases:

- availability bias
- imaginability bias
- representativeness bias
- confirmation bias/positivity bias
- anchoring.

The *availability bias* means that we tend to judge the likelihood of the occurrence of an event on the basis of the ease with which we can bring an instance of it to mind. For example, after the Stardust Fire in Dublin in 1981, there was a much heightened awareness and concern about the likelihood of a similar tragedy happening in other public gathering places like cinemas and theatres, as well as disco halls. The *incidence* of such accidents remained as it had always been (quite low). What had changed was our assessment of the probability of such an accident happening and this was based on the operation of the availability bias. Because of the coverage of the fire and its aftermath, the incident sprang readily to mind for most people at the time, and for some period after. Consequently they were likely to overestimate the probability of such an event occurring again.

The *imaginability bias* has some similarity to availability bias. In the case

---

[4] Evans, J. St B.T (1989) *Bias in Human Reasoning: Causes and Consequences.* Hove and London: Lawrence Erlbaum Associates.

of imaginability bias, our estimate of the likelihood of occurrence of an event is influenced by the ease with which we can imagine the consequence of it. So, for example, if we have a vivid and concrete image of an explosion at a manufacturing plant (perhaps aided by television or newspaper pictures of the scene and some of the injured), we may be inclined to estimate the likelihood of such explosions as higher than their actual statistical incidence. On the other hand, we may underestimate the danger from something like a low level discharge of nuclear energy because we cannot imagine the effects of radiation on the body's internal organs (and this cannot be photographed, although the injuries of someone harmed by a nuclear blast can be seen).

When the *representativeness bias* operates, it means that we believe that a small number of instances of a phenomenon are representative of (i.e. are like) the totality of that phenomenon. To make this clearer, let us look again at the example of the smoker referred to earlier. We noted that it is not uncommon to hear someone who smokes telling of a relative, friend or neighbour who smoked extensively but lived to a ripe old age. This example of just one person is taken as representative of smokers in general. This person's survival is seen as proving that smoking really does not damage health. In the face of this tiny and unrepresentative sample, the results of carefully designed research studies are discounted. Such studies would have been based on *large* and *representative* samples of the population of smokers, matched with a sample of non-smokers on factors like age, sex, diet, exercise taken and general health. Thus their results give a much more comprehensive and detailed picture of the effects of smoking, for men and for women, of pipes, cigars and cigarettes of different levels of tar and nicotine, numbers smoked etc. Such studies also look at quality of health and not just survival rates. But no matter! The representativeness bias tilts the thinking of the layperson towards giving greater emphasis to the small sample of instances of an event or situation that we personally know about than to more distant and abstract facts in a scientific report.

The representativeness bias is also seen in a way of thinking called the *gambler's fallacy*. The layperson's understanding of chance is that possible events should occur in a random order. Imagine for a moment that you are betting on the toss of a coin. What order of heads and tails would you consider random and due to chance alone? Table 5.3 gives you a number of options.

Table 5.3: Some probable sequences of heads and tails in the short term

A	H T T H H H T H T T H T
B	T T T T T T T T T T T T
C	H H H H H H H H H H H T

Most people would choose option A. Yet options B and C can be produced by chance too. The gambler who experiences the sequence in option B will be highly likely to begin betting on heads because she feels that heads are 'due' if the coin has not been tampered with so the 'laws of chance' can operate fairly.

The equivalent to the *gambler's fallacy* is also found in the workplace. A safety advisor told me about the following incident a few years ago.

> An employee had been badly injured when acid splashed in his eyes. In spite of being provided with and cautioned to wear goggles when carrying out the particular procedure, he had not been wearing goggles at the time of the accident. He was off work for a number of months, and at one point there was a real possibility that he would lose his sight. He eventually resumed work and was reassigned to his old job. Sometime later my informant was amazed to see the employee carrying out the procedure which had led to his injuries — without goggles!

To say that my informant was puzzled would be putting it mildly. But this incident seems to be a good example of gambler's fallacy type thinking in action. Having experienced misfortune once, the employee concerned may well have felt that he was unlikely to experience the same bad luck a second time (or perhaps so soon after the first). Just as the gambler in our earlier example felt that it was time for the run of tails to be broken and for heads to appear in the sequence of coin tosses, this employee may have felt that it was beyond the bounds of chance that he would experience a second similar accident. Chance is random, and to most laypeople a random sequence of events will look like option A in Table 5.3.

The mismatch between our idea of chance and how it actually operates is especially noticeable when we focus on the short-term or the immediate situation. The number of times heads and tails will appear if a coin is flipped two thousand times will be very close to 50% for each. However, if the coin is only tossed ten times the number of times heads or tails occurs will be far less likely to be 50%. Yet as researchers Amos Tversky and Daniel Kahneman[5] note, our belief that "the essential characteristics of the process will be represented, not only globally in the entire sequence, but also locally in each of its parts" leads us to expect to see heads and tails in almost equal number in both situations. If we are confronted with a run of heads (or tails) we are inclined to suspect interference from some source. The coin has been tampered with,

[5] Kahneman, D., Slovic, P. and Tversky, A.(Eds.) (1984) *Judgement under Uncertainty: Heuristics and Biases*. Cambridge: Cambridge University Press.

the coin tosser is a magician and is practising sleight of hand, the gods are angry — or we are unlucky.[6]

Confirmation bias arises in our thinking because we have a strong tendency to focus on and process only information that supports our current beliefs. Jonathan Evans[7] holds that confirmation bias is an example of a yet deeper level bias in our thinking. This he calls the *positivity bias*. This bias means that we have difficulty with reasoning formulated in negative terms. For example, if someone said to us "It is not not raining", we would probably have to pause a moment to work out that we were being told that it actually *is* raining. The more usual way of communicating is to say directly what is meant. People who use negative sentence constructions in speech or in writing are often seen as attempting to intimidate, confuse or put one over on their readers or audience.

While the positivity bias works well in most cases in life, it can be the source of human error in certain situations at work. The air crash of a British Midlands flight on its way to Belfast in 1989, known as the M1 crash because of its proximity to that motorway, provides an example of this type of error. The events leading up to the crash were as follows.[8]

The aircraft began to judder. The pilots' first step in their attempt to locate and, if possible, correct the source of the problem was to turn off one of the engines and observe its effect on the juddering. When they did this, the juddering ceased. Reasonably, given the way most people reach decisions in most circumstances, the pilots assumed that they had solved the problem. Their hypothesis was "the problem is in the right-side engine". When the right engine was turned off, the juddering ceased. Therefore they concluded that that was the malfunctioning engine and that by turning it off they had solved the problem. (The plane could be flown on one engine.)

In this case, however, the situation was more complicated. In fact the source of the juddering was the action of the fuel pump attempting to compensate for the malfunction of the engine which was actually at fault, while still serving the sound engine. Once *one* of the engines was switched off (and

---

[6] The link between the representativeness bias and accident proneness discussed in the last chapter will probably have struck you. Our layperson's idea of chance does not include *sequences* of one outcome. Instead we expect random events to fluctuate without any kind of pattern at all. We do not expect a person to have a 'run' of accidents on the basis of chance alone. If this happens, we look for an explanation of it and our tendency is to seek this *within the person* involved. Thus he or she is seen as accident prone when actually the sequence of events we observe is due to chance alone.

[7] Evans, J. St B. T (1989) *op cit.*

[8] Air Accidents Investigation Branch (1990) *Report on the Accident to Boeing 737-400 G-OBME near Kegworth, Leicestershire on January 8, 1989.* Department of Transport, Aircraft Accident Report 4/90. London: HMSO.

in this case, through no fault of the pilots, this was the sound one), the juddering disappeared — not because equipment error had been correctly located and made safe, but because the fuel pump no longer had to serve two engines.

Because people do not normally think in negative terms, the pilots did not test what scientists call the *null hypothesis*. In the M1 case this would mean that as well as saying to themselves, "Suppose it is the right-side engine" and testing it as they did, they would also have said "Suppose it is *not* the right-side engine?" Formulating a null hypothesis like this would have led them to turn the right engine back on and to check the left-side engine — the one that was actually faulty — by turning it off. This procedure would have given the pilots the information that once *one* engine was turned off, the symptom (the juddering) disappeared. It is beyond the scope of this discussion to speculate on what might have followed had they had this information. The example is being used here simply to demonstrate the thinking involved in testing a null hypothesis.

Thinking in this way so that one tests the null hypothesis as well as the hypothesis is extremely uncommon. First, the confirmation bias that inclines us to accept evidence that affirms our ideas without further ado makes us disinclined to probe a situation further. Second, the positivity bias means that even if we were inclined to question the evidence, we have real difficulty in reasoning in the negative and setting about finding data that disconfirms our hypothesis.

Overcoming confirmation and positivity biases requires intensive training and over learning. Only when testing the null hypothesis as well as the more obvious positive hypothesis becomes part of an operator's skill in dealing with a situation will errors arising from confirmation and positivity biases be significantly reduced.

Anchoring is the final kind of thinking bias that can occur when people are making judgements about probability in general. This means that the way a question or information about a topic is framed when it is first introduced influences our subsequent judgements about the topic.

As an example of how anchoring affects probability estimation, let's suppose that we are running a safety campaign to develop safety awareness among the farming community. We want to get farmers and their families to think about the dangers involved in farming and the hazardous nature of various aspects of their workplace (e.g. working alone at a distance from the farmhouse, slurry tanks, machinery etc.). We begin by giving some information on accidents and we use one of two statistics to do so.

In one presentation we point out that one person was killed in a tractor accident in 1994. In another presentation we note that in 1994 seven people were killed through being caught/crushed in machinery.[9] We then ask people

---

[9] Farming in Ireland. *Health and Safety Authority Newsletter*. (1994) No. 83.

to estimate how many fatalities involving slurry pits happened in that year. We find that those who were given the lowest number initially (i.e. one tractor fatality) give a low estimate of the number of slurry pit accidents, while those who were given the higher number (i.e. seven machinery fatalities) give a high estimate of accidents involving slurry. The different starting points resulted in people forming different estimates of the likelihood of the same type of accident. This difference in estimated probability is an example of the effect of anchoring.

Anchoring can lead us to underestimate the degree of danger we are facing as we go about our daily life. We noted in Chapter 2 that the incidence of fatalities in the workplace is actually quite low. This means that if we emphasise fatality statistics in the safety literature — in spite of the seriousness of the loss involved — because the number is low the anchoring effect will tend to lead us to judge the probability of *all* risks as being equally low. So we will be inclined to underestimate the risk of non-fatal but disabling and/or chronically distressing injuries (such as loss of the use of a limb or of the limb itself, chronic pain from an injury, facial scarring etc.).

Obviously policy makers and all those involved in health and safety promotion need to take account of anchoring effects when designing safety education material and information campaigns. We will look again at this issue in Chapter 7.

BUT WILL IT HAPPEN TO ME? JUDGING PROBABILITY IN THE PARTICULAR CASE

When we think about the chances that we ourselves will suffer a loss in a risky situation, additional biasing elements influence our assessment of the situation. As well as the heuristics and biases just discussed, our judgement is affected by whether our exposure to risk is voluntary or not, and the extent to which we believe we can control the ongoing situation or its outcome.

Research on risk perception consistently shows that people accept a higher level of risk for themselves and for others when there is a *voluntary aspect* to getting involved in the situation.[10] This factor probably accounts in part for the participation of some people in high risk sports like parachute jumping, rally driving and rock climbing. In the workplace, this fact would suggest that people who work for themselves (e.g. farmers and self-employed contractors of all kinds) would be inclined to accept higher rates of risk than would people who are employees working at the direction of others. At all events, whatever a person's contract, it appears that being in a position to

---

[10]Fischoff, B., Slovic, P., Lichtenstein, S., Read, S. and Combs, B. (1978) 'How Safe is Safe Enough? A Psychometric Study of Attitudes Towards Technological Risks and Benefits', *Policy Sciences*. 9, pp. 127–52.

choose to run the risk can make a given level of risk more acceptable to the person. This is because choice gives people a sense of having more control over the situation. This sense of control probably reduces the level of dread risk associated with the situation, thus reducing the overall level of risk that is perceived.

Having control, or at least perceiving oneself to have it, is an important influence on our assessment of the probability of an accident happening to ourselves. As well as the control that feeling that we can choose whether or not to engage with or stay in the hazardous situation gives us, our assessment of our level of task related skill also influences our sense of control. If we judge ourselves to be skilful and experienced in the activity involved, we are likely to assess the probability of our being injured — fatally or otherwise — as significantly reduced. Believing that our skill and experience will protect us from accidents, even when the statistical odds are against us, is a common enough illusion. For example, when asked to rate their own level of skill at driving, between 75% and 90% of drivers believed themselves to be safer than the average driver.[11] This estimate obviously bears no relationship to reality, since of course no more than 50% of people can be better than average at any activity.

Even professionals are prone to inaccuracies when judging their own performance. Bus drivers overestimated their skill in driving through narrow gaps (and underestimated their skill in driving through wide ones!).[12] Paramedics trained in resuscitation techniques overestimated their skill in carrying out the procedure some months after the completion of training — 88% felt confident about their ability to apply the procedure, but only 1% actually carried it out correctly.[13]

Estimates of personal control and risk are also affected by the fact of surviving or escaping unhurt from a risky situation. People who have survived or escaped injury rate the situations concerned as less risky, and rate themselves as having more control in those situations than do people who have not experienced such hazards.[14] This fact, coupled with gambler fallacy thinking, may actually result in people who have had accidents becoming less rather than more careful in future.

---

[11] Svenson, O. (1978) 'Risks of Road Transportation in a Psychological Perspective', *Accident Analysis and Prevention.* 10, 267–80.

[12] Cohen, J., Dearnaley, E. J. and Hansel, C. E. M. (1956) 'Risk and Hazard', *Operational Research Quarterly.* 7, (3), pp. 67–82.

[13] Ramirez, A.G., Weaver, F. J., Raizner, A. E., Herrick, K. and Gotto, A.M. (1977) 'The Efficacy of Cardiopulmonary Resuscitation Instruction: An Evaluation', *Public Health.* 67, pp. 1093–5.

[14] Rantanen, J. (1981) 'Risk Assessment and the Setting of Priorities in Occupational Health and Safety', *Scandinavian Journal of Work Environment and Health.* 7, (4), Supplement 4, pp. 84–90.

Perceived skill is not the only element that influences people's feelings of control in a risky situation. Perception of oneself as *lucky* can also affect our actions. Luck in this sense is seen as an attribute of the person, much like an aptitude for mathematics or music. The person sees himself as 'having' luck just as he 'has' these aptitudes. This view of luck is obviously quite different from that involved in locus of control, discussed in the case of repeated accident involvement in Chapter 4. In that case luck had the same meaning as chance, and was seen as a factor external to the individual and not at all as an attribute of the person.

Evidence that some people perceive themselves as lucky and, consequently, more or less independent of the laws of chance, comes from studies of gamblers.[15] It is likely that similar thinking underlies the actions of some employees, although there is a need for research specifically designed to test this hypothesis.

THE STORY SO FAR . . .

In the ordinary course of events, people assess risk using heuristics — very general rules based on their impression of the situation. Their thinking is heavily influenced by factors like the availability of information about specific hazards, the imaginability of the hazard and/or its consequences and their idea of how probability should operate (representativeness). The way information on risk is first presented (the anchoring bias), and people's tendency to word hypotheses in positive terms and not to question information which seems to support their hypotheses any further (positivity and confirmation biases), also have an influence.

Even where risk in a situation is generally judged to be high, people may still assess the risk to themselves as low. This is usually because they see themselves as being sufficiently skilled, experienced or lucky to be able to run the risk and survive unscathed.

Nor is this the end of the story of the layperson's assessment of risk! Factors other than the person's estimate of the likelihood that his or her actions will end in loss also affect risk taking behaviour. These are discussed next.

---

[15]Heslin, J. M. (1967) 'Craps and Magic', *American Journal of Sociology*. 73, 316–30; Langer, E. J. (1975) 'The Illusion of Control', *Journal of Personality and Social Psychology*. 32, (2), pp. 311–28.

THE IMPACT ON RISK TAKING OF FACTORS OTHER THAN PROBABILITY

Even though people may believe that they are running a significant risk in carrying out a particular activity, they may still engage in it. The factors which lead to this state of affairs are usually social and organisational in nature. They can range from the apparently trivial (such as feeling that the PPE supplied makes a person look silly) to the very significant (seeing the experts as lacking in credibility and questioning their expertise).

Reasons why employees take risks with their health and safety at work fall into four main categories. These are:

1. Inconvenience — if PPE and/or other health and safety gear is not readily to hand the extra effort needed to fetch it may deter people from doing so.[16] (This point links back to the discussion of effort in Chapter 3.) Safety equipment is sometimes uncomfortable to wear and/or awkward to use.[17] The inconvenience this causes the individual may again deter her from wearing it.

2. Interference — if PPE or other safety equipment is poorly designed it may interfere with getting the job done. For example, a machine may operate more slowly or take longer to set up if the safety guard is on. This may affect earnings if pay is linked to productivity. The employee is inclined to take the risk of not wearing PPE or of disabling the safety feature of equipment in order to protect earnings.[18]

3. Image — apart from the comfort and interference aspects, following safety regulations may have a negative effect on how a person is regarded by co-workers. In a now classic report on PPE and image, researchers found that the perception of the safety conscious employee who wore PPE was not a flattering one. This negative image was shared by managers as well as other employees. Managers saw the wearer as reliable and conscientious but also slow and not very bright intellectually. Employees believed that workers who wore PPE were seen by other employees as "sissies".[19]

---

[16]Laner, S. (1959) 'Some Factors for and against Acceptance of Safety Footwear by Steelworkers'. London: *Report from the Human Factors Section, Operations Research Department, British Iron and Steel Research Association*; Booth, R. T. (1976) 'Machinery Guarding', *Engineering*. December Issue. Technical File 36.

[17]Feeney, R.J. (1986) 'Why is There Resistance to Wearing Protective Equipment at Work? Possible Strategies for Overcoming This', *Journal of Occupational Accidents*. 8, pp. 207–213.

[18]*Ibid.*

[19]Pirani, M. and Reynolds, J. (1976) 'Gearing up for Safety – or These Boots Were Made for Walking', *Personnel Management*. Feburary. pp. 25–29.

4. Belief — running a risk is influenced by the beliefs that people hold about their options in the work situation. For example, if an employee believes that *not* accepting the risk inherent in a job could result in being sacked or made redundant in an economy where jobs are scarce, he will be unlikely to refuse to carry out a task, even when it involves a risk that he would prefer not to take.[20] In a similar vein, if employees believe that their chances of promotion are linked to doing a risky job without complaint, they will accept risk. In cases where "danger money" is paid (less provocative terms for this, such as "bonus for unsocial conditions" may be used), an employee may run the risk involved in order to increase earnings. Beliefs may affect safety related behaviour in another way also. A number of researchers describe the *credibility gap* which can exist between technical experts and the members of the public[21] (which of course includes employees). If people are not convinced of the expertise of specialists, they may not follow their advice because they do not believe the recommended safety and health promotion procedures will work. This has been found to be the case with wearing safety helmets on construction sites, for example.[22]

These four topics all relate to the *social* and *organisational* aspects of the workplace. The purchase of PPE and equipment is an organisational issue. Managers can choose to pay as much attention to the safety relevant aspect of PPE, production equipment, workstations etc. as to their cost in financial terms. Thus purchasing PPE which is comfortable to wear, easy to work in (so that earnings and job satisfaction are not adversely effected), and which employees do not feel makes them look foolish or silly in some way are key elements in risk reduction.

Decoupling decisions about hiring, deploying and terminating employees' contracts from safety issues, such as reporting unsafe equipment or work practices, and not requiring personnel to accept above-average risk as a rou-

[20] Walters, V. and Haines, T. (1988) 'Workers' Perceptions, Knowledge and Responses Regarding Occupational Health and Safety: A Report on a Canadian Study', *Social Science and Medicine*. 27, (11), pp. 1189–96.

[21] Fischoff, B., Slovic, P. and Lichtenstein, S. *'The Public' versus 'The Experts': Perceived versus Actual Disagreements about Risks* Proceedings of the 20th International Congress of Applied Psychology, Edinburgh, July 1982; Vlek, C. and Stallen, P-J. (1981) 'Judging Risks and Benefits in the Small and in the Large', *Organisational Behaviour and Human Performance*. 28, pp. 235–271; Lindell, M. K. and Barnes, V. E. (1986) 'Protective Response to Technological Emergency: Risk Perception and Behavioural Intention', *Nuclear Safety*. 27, (4), pp. 457–67.

[22] Hickling, E.M. (1985) 'An Investigation on Construction Sites of Factors Affecting the Acceptability and Wearing of Safety Helmets', *Report for the Health and Safety Executive*. Institute for Consumer Ergonomics, Loughborough University of Technology. Report No. G394.

tine aspect of their job is a key organisational element in controlling workplace risk. All managers should be seen to follow this practice.

Wearing PPE and following safety procedures, like running equipment with guards on, have a *social* as well as an organisational aspect. Peer influence is a crucial element in human behaviour. Few people can work side-by-side with others each day without being affected by the opinions and perceptions of their co-workers. Where attitudes to working safely are negative, and where behaving safely is considered wimpish or seen as currying favour with the boss, the pressure will be on the individual employees to conform to the group norm and take risks, even if these are against their own better judgement. Safety managers and policy makers cannot afford to dismiss this aspect of human behaviour. They must accept it and work with the workforce to create a culture where the norm is to behave safely.

Communication between employees and safety advisors and experts is a further key area for action. It is as important that employees can read and evaluate the reports of research on safety as it is that safety managers and advisors, managers generally and other professionals can. As we are seeing in this book, there are no simple, single dimension answers to improving workplace safety. When such unidimensional and simple answers are given to complex problems, and are then shown not to work, people are inclined to dismiss *all* safety information as irrelevant. Education in understanding the technical aspects of safety, which includes an understanding of the psychological issues involved, is an essential part in developing a safer workplace.

Chapter 6

Human Error and Designing for Safety

A wrong rule — scaffolding erected without a guardrail behind the employees

HOW COULD IT HAVE HAPPENED?

On 8 January 1989, a British Airways flight crashed just off the M1 motorway as it attempted an emergency landing at East Midlands airport. Forty-seven people lost their lives. The emergency was precipitated by the apparent failure of one of the engines of the Boeing 401 plane, the most up-to-date model in Boeing's 400 series at that time. The enquiry into the accident showed that the pilots had turned off the healthy engine and were flying on the faulty engine at the time of the crash.

On the face of it the M1 crash must rank among the more incomprehensible of air disasters.[1] How could two experienced pilots have turned off the wrong engine? What does it mean to say — as the enquiry concluded — that the crash was due to "pilot error"? What is the nature of human error anyway? How, if at all, might it be prevented from occurring or from having disastrous consequences? These issues are the focus of this chapter.

HUMAN ERROR AND SYSTEM DESIGN

Errors in human performance can occur when there is a mismatch between the way the human mind processes information and the way a work system operates.[2] In order to fully grasp how this mismatch can arise and how it can result in human error, it is necessary to understand some of the key principles of human cognition.

Cognition is the *activity of knowing*.[3] The aspects of human cognition which are most important for understanding the nature of human error are the processes of selective attending, information handling and judging and evaluating. Since cognition is one of the most complex aspects of human behaviour, considering the processes involved in it and how they can result in human error will also be complex. Discussions of human error often play down any such notion of complexity. Instead the impression is given that the error would never have occurred if the operator had not been deficient in some way. Quite often the implication is that she has simply been careless or negligent. The message of this chapter is that, contrary to this point of view, human error is seldom a simple matter of either negligence or personal weakness. More often than not its roots lie in the mismatch between the way in which we humans process information and the way in which the work system is designed and/or managed. Only when designers and managers know about and understand the principles of cognition discussed here will they be able to appreciate the true nature of human error. Only then will they be in a position to create and operate safer work systems.

---

[1] Air Accidents Investigation Branch (1990) *Report on the Accident to Boeing 737-400 G-OBME near Kegworth, Leicestershire on January 8, 1989*. Department of Transport, Aircraft Accident Report 4/90, London: HMSO.

[2] The term 'work system' is used here to cover all workplaces — farms, factories, construction sites, ships, offices, and settings like schools, hospitals, libraries etc. A work system has both a technical and an organisational aspect. Human error can arise from either source, e.g. because of badly designed (ergonomically wrong) equipment or because of a management style and organisational climate which, for example, gives rise to stress.

[3] Neisser, U. (1976) *Cognition and Reality*. New York: Freeman & Co.

KEY ASPECTS OF HUMAN COGNITION

Selective Attending

We need to be able to process information *selectively* in order to survive. Each instant of each day our mind receives a flood of information through our senses. Sights, sounds, smells and tastes flow in upon us. We are constantly receiving information from our body about its external and internal state. This tells us whether we are sitting comfortably or not, whether we have injured ourselves, whether the temperature is too hot, too cold or just right, whether we have a headache, backache or indigestion. If we became conscious of *all* the information available through our senses at once, our information processing capacity would be overloaded. We would be psychologically paralysed and would be unable to take any kind of action at all. Overload and paralysis of action can happen because our cognitive capacity for processing information at any particular point of time is limited.

The capacity of a person's *working memory* at any one time is approximately seven chunks of information, plus or minus two chunks.[4] A *chunk* of information is defined as "the highest level integration of the stimulus material available to a person".[5] When information is chunked, single bits of information are organised into meaningful units. For example, as you read this sentence you are not processing each single letter on the page. You are at the very least processing chunks of letters (words) and each word may have many more than seven or even more than nine letters in it. (The word "processing" has ten letters.) Chunking allows us to handle very large amounts of information indeed. This is because each chunk holds tens and perhaps even hundreds of single bits of information. The *size* of the chunk is not limited, although the *number* of chunks active in our working memory at any given time is limited to an average of seven with a range from five to nine. The key factor in all of this is that the individual bits of information *within* each chunk are organised into meaningful units.[6] If a person can create connections be-

---

[4] Logie, R.H. (1999) 'Working Memory', *The Psychologist*. 12, (4), 174–8; Miller, G. (1956) 'The Magical Number Seven Plus or Minus Two: Some Limits in our Capacity for Processing Information', *Psychological Review*. 63, 81–97.

[5] Simon, H.A. (1975) 'How Big is a Chunk?', *Science*. 183, pp. 482–8.

[6] The difference in cognitive capacity which we see between an expert chess player and a novice at the game is a good example of what a 'chunk' of information is and how chunking can affect performance. To the novice, *each* of the thirty-two pieces on the board is a single chunk of information. The average novice player can concentrate on an average of seven pieces at a time. As a result the novice's capacity to anticipate the moves of a more skilled opponent is severely limited. The pattern created by all thirty-two pieces forms just one chunk for the chess master, leaving on average six free chunks of working memory capacity available. As a result the chess expert can more easily anticipate the moves of an opponent and outwit them.

tween the different bits of information she has on a topic, the number of chunks needed to think and problem-solve regarding that topic will be decreased. As result of freeing up some chunks, the person will have expanded working memory capacity. (As you can see, human cognition is indeed complex! But if you take the time to grasp it, you will have a better understanding of the human side of safety.)

The term *working memory* is used by psychologists to talk about the processes involved when a person is actively attending to a task and is drawing on past experience to deal with it. For example, when you are reading a newspaper you are drawing on your remembered knowledge of recent events and personalities to help you to understand and think about what you read. The psychological process of *selective attending* protects working memory from overload by distributing our limited processing capacity only among the aspects of the situation which we believe are critical for performing the task on hand.

As you may have guessed, this state of affairs means that we are not consciously aware of most of the information that reaches our senses. Generally we are unaware of the ticking of the clock on the wall, of the hum of a machine or traffic in the background, of the dog barking in the distance or of the birds squabbling outside the window. Only when our attention is drawn to these things — perhaps by my writing about them here, or when you are waiting for the clock to strike or its alarm to go off, for example — do we notice them.

As an example of how selective attending operates, think back to a situation where you were at a meeting or party and were talking with a colleague or acquaintance. You were immersed in discussion with that person, but suddenly you found yourself trying to hear what people a few feet away were talking about. You may have heard them mention your name or a topic that was important to you. So, although you would be unable to say what they were discussing an instant before, you suddenly found yourself very aware of their conversation. Psychologists call this the *cocktail party phenomenon* and its is a prime example of how selective attending works. While you were *consciously* focused on the conversation you were involved in, you were simultaneously processing the flow of information around you at a *subliminal* (or subthreshold) level. As long as it appeared irrelevant to you and your interests, the information was not consciously processed. However, when it became relevant to you it became the focus of your active attention in working memory.

See DeGroot, A. D. (1965) *Thought and Choice in Chess*. The Hague: Mouton, for a more detailed discussion of the difference between chess masters and other players.

Selective Attending and Human Error

Selective attending relates to the occurrence of error in the following ways. First, people at work selectively attend to what they believe to be the critical aspects of the task on hand. If the aspects they believe to be important are *not* so, then the likelihood of error is high. Good training is the way to prevent this situation.

Good training means more than just teaching the person what the job involves and how to do it. It includes giving full and accurate information on those aspects of the situation that are safety critical. This ensures that the employee has a clear grasp of the process involved and does not misunderstand the significance of different kinds of equipment or system malfunction. The discovery of safety critical elements and how to deal with them should not be left to guesswork or be learned from mistakes made on the job.

Second, based on their formal job training and what they have learned from experience in doing the job, people build up a *schema* or working model of the job on hand. This schema includes the knowledge the person has about the important and safety critical elements of the task. When working on the task the person will naturally pay more attention to these elements than to those that training and experience suggest are less important. If it should happen that one or more of the other 'less important' elements becomes critical for the safe performance of the task, it is highly likely that the person will fail to notice them. In this event the likelihood of human error is again high.

The solution in this case is a design one. If an element in a piece of equipment or a system develops a fault, its defective status should be immediately and clearly signalled to the operator. The designer's aim is to mimic the cocktail party phenomenon by breaking into the selective attending process to *grab* the person's conscious information processing capacity in working memory. A signal that is distinctive and intense will do this. Buzzers, hooters and flashing lights are among the kinds of signals that can be used to grab attention. The best kind of signal to use will depend upon the working conditions prevailing at a particular site or workstation. Among the issues to be considered when choosing a signal are whether the environment is quiet or noisy and whether the operator is likely to be looking in the direction of the signal or not. (Information on choosing the best signal for a given work situation can be obtained from standard ergonomic engineering textbooks and from Health and Safety Authority information sheets.)

INFORMATION HANDLING

Once a person is engaged with a situation, information about it can be handled in either of two ways. These are controlled information processing and automatic information processing.

Controlled information processing is used when the situation requires the person's full attention during performance. This can be the case when:

- the task is a new one and the person has not yet built up a level of expertise in doing it

- the task is a complex one and even an expert needs to continue to give it full attention

- the task is a familiar one but something unusual has happened and the person has to think about it in order to solve the problem.

Controlled information gathering is slow and is done serially or step-by-step. It takes effort and requires that the person concentrates all of his information processing resources upon it.

Automatic information processing is used when the situation is familiar and the person has developed a good level of skill in dealing with it. It is no longer necessary to give one's full attention continuously to the details of the task. Generally a number of elements of the task can be performed simultaneously and often the person can be involved in a second, quite different task. This is known as *parallel processing of information* and it contrasts with the serial (step-by-step) processing that is a feature of controlled information handling. Automatic processing requires less effort than controlled processing.

Car Driving and the Two Types of Information Handling

When you first drive a car you use controlled processing. You are aware of each element of the task from putting on your seatbelt and putting the key in the ignition, to starting the engine, clutching and putting the car in gear, to finally achieving a smooth take-off while keeping an eye on your rear-view mirror and checking your blind spot as you pull out.

Because controlled processing is required, the learner driver will find the experience effortful. Working memory will be loaded to and indeed beyond its seven (plus or minus two) chunk limit. Processing capacity will be focused on driving and the learner will have no spare capacity for small talk with the instructor or for thinking about other aspects of his life. Processing is serial and consequently each element of the task is dealt with in sequence rather than in parallel. This means that there will be poor co-ordination between those parts of driving which must be performed in tandem. For example, declutching and letting off the handbrake must be smoothly co-ordinated in a hill start. As you know, stalling of engines and jerky take-offs are notable characteristics of a learner driver's performance, whether on the flat or on hills!

Contrast this state of affairs with what happens once the person has acquired the skill of driving. Much of his performance is done by automatic processing. This means that performance will be relatively fast and a number of elements of the task will be performed in parallel rather than sequentially. For example, the skilled driver will pull out smoothly, declutching and letting off the handbrake while monitoring the state of traffic in the vicinity. Skilled drivers do not have to devote all of their conscious attention and working memory capacity to each element of the task of driving (unless conditions are hazardous or unusual in some way). As a result they will be able to think about the meeting they are going to, listen to the car radio or carry on a conversation with a passenger without their driving being affected in any major way. This is possible because many of the elements of which the skill of driving is composed have become melded together to form a single chunk of information in the skilled driver's schema or model of driving. The result is that driving now requires less working memory capacity and the spare capacity can be used for other activities.

INFORMATION HANDLING AND HUMAN ERROR

Errors During Controlled Processing

A number of different types of errors can arise when information handling is being done in the controlled mode. First, *information overload* with *consequent load shedding* of data can arise in very complex task situations where multi-tasking, or doing a number of things at once, is required of the person. As noted earlier, controlled processing is effortful and takes up much, if not all, of a person's information handling resources. Consequently he will have little or no cognitive capacity available to deal with other demands that may arise. Therefore there is a danger of error if the situation is a complicated one with many and changing requirements. In such a high demand situation the person can very easily become cognitively overloaded. Selective attending will come into operation to protect against this overload. Some information will be offloaded. If this data is critical to safe performance, errors will occur.

To avoid errors due to offloading critical data, engineers and systems designers must ensure that the cognitive load on operators working in safety critical situations remains within the limits of working memory. The safest design will restrict cognitive load to five chunks of information at any one time. As you now know, five chunks is the lower limit of working memory capacity. By not exceeding this level of load, the designer is creating a situation with which most properly trained and experienced operators will be able to cope.

The second category of errors which can arise during controlled information processing are *rule based errors*. Rules give us the procedures that are to be followed in particular situations. As such they are useful in managing cognitive load. Once we have identified the problem, and provided we know the rule to apply in the situation, the rule tells us how we should proceed. Two types of errors can arise when using rules:

- a rule which is usually appropriate to the situation is wrong this time, so applying it results in an error. This type of error happens in controlled processing when the person jumps to the conclusion that the current situation is similar to situations in the past when the rule did apply. Because of some surface similarity between the two instances, the person does not examine the current problem closely. As a result an error is made because the rule which usually works is inappropriate on this occasion. Responding incorrectly to a fire in an electrical appliance is an example of this type of error. It is usually correct to use water to put out a fire. However, if the source of the fire is electrical, using a stream of water from a hose or pouring water onto the fire from a bucket can result in the electrocution of the person involved.[7] In the case of an electrical fire following a usually good rule results in disaster

- the second type of rule based error occurs when the rule itself, and thus the procedure it advocates, is wrong. This can be the case when a person is incorrectly trained. The person follows the rule, but because the rule is wrong, the person makes an error. For example, erecting scaffolding without base plates may be the 'rule' or accepted practice in a particular construction company. New recruits are shown this unsafe technique when they join. The procedure itself is an unsafe one and, if not corrected, will result in an incident or accident sooner or later. The cause of the incident or accident may then be put down to a human error made by the person who erected the scaffolding. Closer examination of the circumstances would show that the error really happened because the person was following a bad rule.

So what steps can be taken to reduce the likelihood of occurrence of rule based errors? Obviously risky practices should be guarded against during training (whether this is on or off the job). It also follows that supervisors and members of a workforce should be vigilant in case bad rules become part of the work practices of a company or a work group within it. The principles of behaviour covered in Chapter 3 apply to this situation.

Guarding against errors due to the misapplication of a good rule requires

---

[7] In these cases the water acts as a conductor of electricity back to the person. Proper fire control arrangements would ensure that one of the substances (ABC, CO_2 or DC), which can be safely used on electrical and all other kinds of fires, would be to hand. If water is the only thing available, the person should throw the bucket containing the water onto the fire. Water should never be poured onto an electrical fire from a bucket or hose.

first that people be made aware of the possibility of their making such errors. For example, the information in this chapter should not be seen as relevant only to supervisors and those who have responsibility for safety with an organisation, nor should it be kept as the special knowledge of the safety consultant or expert on human error. Information on the nature of human error and how to minimise it should be part of the safety training that *all* employees receive. In this way operators themselves can be alert to the need to work with extra caution in circumstances where the misapplication of a good rule may be likely.[8]

The second step is to train operators to carry out an appropriateness check in safety critical situations. Thus where the results of an error would be costly in terms of loss of life, injury, lost time and/or financial or product loss, special training in checking the applicability of a rule should be given. The rule appropriateness check should be built into the work routine so that it becomes part of the normal procedure for the particular task. Thus the good rule will be less likely to be misapplied, even when cognitive load on the operator is high.

Finally, engineers and systems designers should design to control for this type of rule based error where possible. For example, it may be possible to prevent the misapplication of a good rule by locking the mechanism when the conditions for the appropriate application of the rule are not met. It thus becomes impossible for the operator to apply the rule inappropriately. Figure 6.1 illustrates what is involved here.

In the figure, the valve will open only when all of the conditions for the application of the rule are met.

Errors During Automatic Processing

Errors made during the automatic processing of information are known as *skill based errors*.[9] They fall into two main categories.

The first group of skill based errors are due to *over attention* on the part of the person. You can get some sense of what this involves if you imagine explaining how you drive a car to someone else. You will almost certainly omit steps from the sequence, repeat some steps and reverse the order of others. This will happen because once knowledge becomes automated, as it is in the case of the skilled worker (or car driver), bringing it under controlled processing which can lead to performance breakdown. Some or all of the three kinds of slips or lapses just mentioned will be made.

---

[8] Awareness of the possibility of making this type of error will not *of itself* prevent this kind of error being made. As will be explained, training in checking the applicability of a rule must also be given, and where possible the system should be designed in a way which *requires* such a check to be made.

[9] Reason, J. (1990) *Human Error*. Cambridge: Cambridge University Press.

Figure 6.1: Lock out valve prevents mischarge if additive is wrong

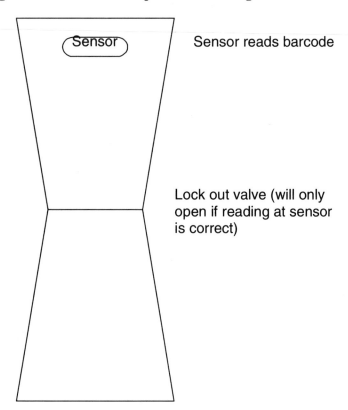

Sensor reads barcode

Lock out valve (will only
open if reading at sensor
is correct)

Errors due to over attention can arise when supervision is intrusive. Having a supervisor looking over your shoulder, as it were, and perhaps asking questions such as "What's happening there?", will interrupt the smooth flow of performance. Minimising these kinds of errors requires a supervisory policy that is not overly intrusive on the operator.

The second category of skill based errors are due to *inattention*. By definition automated information handling does not involve closely attending to the details of task performance. Indeed, the fact that it does not is one of the signs that skill has been developed. As we saw earlier, automated processing has the bonus of freeing cognitive capacity to deal with other tasks or aspects of the work situation. The downside of highly skilled performance is that strongly established habitual responses can come into operation in situations where they are not appropriate.

Because of surface similarities between a well known task and some aspect of the current situation, a *strong but wrong* response can be executed before the person realises that the demands of this particular situation are different in some safety critical way. Driving in icy conditions provides an example of this kind of error. Braking is the well practised response to feeling one's car going out of control. Braking is an inappropriate response when skidding on ice — instead the drive is supposed to go with the skid and steer the car to safety. In this particular case, braking is an example of a strong but wrong habitual response.

The similarity between this kind of error and the rule based error involving the misapplication of a usually good rule during controlled processing will probably have struck you. The difference between the two kinds of errors lies in the person's degree of awareness of the situation. Where rule based errors are concerned, the person is consciously thinking about the task and deciding on a particular course of action. The misapplication of the rule is a mistake. Had she realised the true nature of the problem, the person would have acted differently. When a strong but wrong error is made, the person has acted without thinking. This should not be read as meaning that the person was culpable. Remember the essence of automated information handling is that little or no active information processing is involved or indeed is required. The person acts from habit in this case, whereas she has acted on the basis of a misapplication of information when applying a rule inappropriately.

Since errors due to strong but wrong habits are errors of inattention to now critical aspects of a task, it will not surprise you to hear that strategies for reducing these kinds of errors are similar to those discussed in the earlier section on selective attending. There we noted that people will usually pay attention to those aspects of a situation which training, experience and belief tells them are important. Aspects which appear to be less important are not processed in order to protect our working memory from overload. This can mean that an operator will simply not notice if circumstances change so that one or some of these aspects of the situation are now crucial to safety. So, as suggested earlier, equipment should be designed to grab the person's attention and move them from the automatic to controlled mode of information processing when operating conditions become safety critical.

Once attention has been grabbed and the person is actively attending to the situation, she must be able to diagnose the problem correctly and take appropriate action. Equipment or system design can help here also by indicating the nature of the current problem on the apparatus or system status display. Writing about the Three Mile Island nuclear reactor breakdown at Harrisburg in 1979, Charles Perrow[10] emphasises the necessity to make systems *less opaque* and *more transparent* so that operators can have a clear understanding of the nature and location of a problem when it arises. Signal-

---

[10]Perrow, C. (1984) *Normal Accidents*. New York: Basic Books

ling that there is a problem without also indicating what it is, and what and where corrective action needs to be taken, may not give enough support to an operator in a safety critical crisis situation. As in all cases discussed so far, training and practice in dealing with the problem once it is diagnosed are an essential part of minimising the likelihood of human error.

JUDGING AND EVALUATING

Judging and evaluating information received is a fundamental part of decision making. Decision making is done in the controlled mode of information handling. As we saw in the last chapter, human decision making is not an entirely logical and reasoned process of reviewing, weighing and rationally balancing all of the information available, and eventually coming to a decision on the basis of the facts of the matter. This is because our limited working memory capacity requires that we selectively attend to those aspects of the situation that appear to be most relevant and critical to dealing with it.

Herbert Simon[11] discussed the effect of the limitation of human information processing on decision making in his *theory of bounded rationality*, for which he was awarded the Nobel Prize in Economics in 1978. Prior to Simon's examination of how people actually make decisions, a theory known as *subjective expected utility theory* (SEU) had been used by economists and others to guide their investigations of how people make choices. SEU theory made a number of assumptions about the nature of human cognition. The assumption which is relevant to this discussion of human error is that decision makers are able to have a clear and comprehensive view of all the alternative courses of action available to them in a given situation — and the outcomes of these alternative actions. Psychologists who have researched the nature and functioning of working memory have shown repeatedly that this assumption is not justified. Simon points this out and explains that instead people settle for a course of action that is tolerable to them in the immediate term. He calls this *satisficing*. Satisficing is defined as the tendency to settle for a satisfactory rather than ideal course of action.

As well as being constrained by the effects of bounded rationality, people's judgement and evaluation of events is influenced by the reasoning bias we discussed in relation to personal risk assessment in the last chapter. You will remember that there we discussed the role of confirmation bias in the M1 crash. We noted the importance of training people to counteract this bias in their thinking. Here we will look at how attention to instrument display design could have helped overcome confirmation bias.

---

[11] Simon, H.A. (1983) *Reason in Human Affairs*. London: Basil Blackwell.

In that accident the healthy engine was switched off and the plane was flown on the faulty engine. This was possible as long as no extra strain was exerted on that engine. However, as the plane began descending to make its emergency landing, the faulty engine could no longer function and effectively self-destructed. The pilots had found that, when they switched off *one* of the engines, the juddering, which was the only symptom they had to judge by, disappeared. Their 'hypothesis' — that the right-side engine was at fault — appeared to be confirmed. Psychologically confirmation bias operated and they were led to believe that they had dealt with the problem correctly. In fact, they had made an incorrect decision. The fact that no aspect of the instrument display in the cockpit clearly or in an attention grabbing manner indicated the damage status of the engine which was actually faulty, is an example of how system design could have helped to reduce the likelihood of an accident apparently due to human error. If engine status had been clearly and prominently displayed on the instrument panel, then there would have been much less opportunity for confirmation bias to occur in dealing with the emergency.

When a fault develops in a piece of equipment, the location and nature of the fault should be clearly displayed to the operator. Given our tendency to confirmation and positivity biases, the less judging and evaluating of obscure, incomplete and unfamiliar data that the operator has to do, the better from the safety point of view.

A lot of ground has been covered in this chapter and some of the material has been quite complex. Table 6.1 summarises the types of human errors discussed and notes the action that must be taken to either reduce the likelihood of their occurrence or minimise their detrimental effects.

SAFER BY DESIGN

The first thing to note about this section is its title. Absolute safety of a piece of equipment, a work system or a workplace cannot be guaranteed. Instead we must talk about steps which engineers and designers can take to make the equipment, systems and work settings that they create *safer* to be in and to operate.

There are two aspects to the design of safer work systems. First are the *technical* or *ergonomic* aspects. Many of these have already been discussed in tandem with the types of human error that they help to prevent. *Policy issues* concerning the financial cost of designing safer systems must also be considered. Both of these matters are dealt with below.

Table 6.1: Summary of types of human error, their psychological base and minimisation strategies

Type of error	Psychological base	Minimisation strategy
Person misses 'key' piece of information/ data	a. Selective attending b. Experience based cognitive schema led person to miss an unexpected/unusual fault	Explain safety critical aspects of process and system Eliminate guess work Override schema by designing to grab person's attention
During controlled processing		
Load shedding	Information overload of working memory in complex or multi-tasking situations	Design safety critical complex equipment to minimise load on working memory Look at staffing levels so individuals do not become so loaded
Applies the wrong rule this time	Experience based cognitive schema leads person to apply the wrong rule in this situation	Increase person's awareness of this cognitive tendency Build a rule appropriateness check into performance during training Design to prevent the misapplication of this rule
Incorrect practice — the rule is always wrong	Bad practice is learned during training or picked up through modelling bad example	Best practice during training Leading by good example
During automatic processing		
Performance breakdown — actions omitted, actions performed in wrong order	Over attention due to moving back to controlled mode	Non-intrusive supervision
Wrong action performed as a 'strong but wrong' response	Automated habit based action	Design to grab attention Design to show nature of problem and the required action

	Cognitive biases	
Misinterpretation of information — under-estimating some risks and over-estimating others	Various cognitive biases	Give information to all staff on the existence and nature of these biases Specific training to overcome e.g. con-firmation/positivity biases, effects of anchoring Present information in ways that allow for these biases

Technical/Ergonomic Aspects of Safer Design

The main ergonomic issues in design concern how to give necessary and sufficient information to operators in a form that they can easily grasp, and how to facilitate their dealing with the situation swiftly and accurately. The following points summarise and supplement those discussed in earlier sections of this chapter.

Good design requires that we:

- support and supplement the operators' knowledge by putting important task relevant information on, in or near the apparatus, workstation or bench

- give operators immediate feedback on the results of their actions

- build on the associations between objects and their use which users have learned through experience in school, home and other work and non-work settings

- devise equipment so that unsafe actions are impossible or highly effortful to perform

- plan error tolerant equipment and systems that allow recovery from human error.

Let's look at each of these points in more detail.

Provision of task relevant information

Putting important, task relevant information that supports and supplements the knowledge of the operator in the immediate vicinity of the worker involves two steps. First, it is necessary to make the ongoing working of the system visible so that the operator can easily check his or her mental model of the process against the actual state of affairs. Second, critical information should be displayed clearly and in a way that does not overload the operator. Safe operation of equipment requires that the operator has no less, but also no more, information than she or he requires when necessary.

Safety critical information should be placed at the centre of the information display. Its status should be clearly indicated — for example, by having the danger zone on a dial clearly marked out from the safe area. If the process becomes critical, the operator's attention should be grabbed and directed towards the relevant aspect of the display by a combination of sound and visual signals (e.g. a buzzer to grab attention in combination with a flashing light on the critical part of the display).

Outcome feedback

Feedback on the outcome of the operator's actions is essential for efficient and effective performance. The results of the operator's action should be immediately and clearly displayed. Letting the operator see the results of action taken reduces uncertainty and anxiety. It prevents possibly dangerous overreaction, and it reduces delay in taking further corrective action where this is necessary.

Associations between objects and their use

Mappings and *affordances* are technical terms for the natural associations or links formed between objects in our environment and our way of using them. For example, a round door *knob* affords or suggests turning, while the affordance associated with a door *handle* suggests that the way to use it is to press down on it.

Engineers and designers should use existing associations between objects and people's responses to them. They should be particularly careful *not* to require people to use controls in novel ways when safety depends on the speed and accuracy of their response.

Making unsafe actions effortful

People *will* make errors. Where errors are critical for safety, designers and engineers should work with psychologists to determine the kind of error the operator may make. They should then prevent the error by designing the equipment with a fail-safe element which will not allow the system to be operated in an unsafe or risky way.

You may well be thinking of situations where operators disable guards on equipment. In Chapters 3 and 5 we noted that people generally do not like making efforts which they judge to be unnecessary or disproportionate to the risk involved. To overcome the problem of people disabling fail-safe devices, designers must capitalise on our tendency to conserve effort and make it effortful for people to behave in unsafe ways. For example, it should be more difficult and effortful to disengage a guard on a piece of equipment than to operate it with the guard in place.

Error tolerant equipment and error retrieval

To err is human ... so designers must allow for error retrieval in critical situations. This means that the occurrence of an error must not immediately result in an injury to the operator or loss of product. Designing for error retrieval requires that systems be made error tolerant — we must accept that they can never be error free.

Designing an error tolerant system involves the following steps:

- identifying the critical aspects of the process where, if an error occurs, injury, loss or life, loss or product or an incident like a pollution accident will occur

- analysing the work situation and aspects of the operation relating to critical parts of the process to determine the kind of human error that is likely to be made

- designing or modifying the operating system or piece of equipment to signal to the operator that a mistake has been made and to allow recovery from that mistake.

POLICY ISSUES IN SAFER DESIGN

For many of us, our attitude to safety is sometimes rather like that imputed to Saint Augustine on the matter of chastity — "Yes, but not just yet". The issue is often couched in terms of the costs of designing safer work systems or of modifying existing ones to make them safer. The costs of safety are declared to be prohibitive because they make companies uncompetitive, thus leading eventually to job loss. As we noted in Chapter 1, economists' analyses of the costs arising from poor or no wastage and loss control, and from the uninsured and uninsurable aspects of accidents, show that this argument is not valid in financial terms.

In terms of the psychology of working safely, some general points on safety policy should be considered. As will be evident from reading the preceding section on the technical aspects of safer system design, the identification of psychological hazards and their removal is no more exceptional a design activity than is the identification of electronic, mechanical, chemical or other technical hazards. It is simply different because it requires the involvement of a different discipline — psychology — in addition to engineering. Otherwise the aim is the same — to design an effective production system.

Classical ergonomics, which focused on eliminating any mismatch between the human body and the equipment used, is a well established subdiscipline of engineering. Cognitive ergonomics, which aims to eliminate mismatch between the way in which people process information and the information carrying aspects of the work environment, needs to become equally well established if modern technology is to be used in a cost effective way. The link between good design, safer design and efficient and effective design is straightforward when one thinks about it.

The aim in all cases is to design a system where avoidable costs (such as those arising from human error due to poor system design) *are* avoided. Work systems which are designed and operated in ways that take human error into account are more cost effective on a number of counts than are those which ignore this aspect of operator performance. For example, errors that are retrievable mean less loss of product and the costs involved therein can be avoided. Where errors cannot be retrieved, the company incurs the costs of the raw material used in the aborted production or in the defective units produced.

Production time is lost when errors occur because they slow down performance. This may have a direct consequence for meeting a supply deadline. There will also be an indirect cost to the enterprise since its overheads (heating, lighting, administration etc.) are only defrayed if operating costs from inefficiencies are kept to a minimum. In sum, in the modern business environment the psychological aspects of good workplace design are not *niceties* — they are *necessities*.

Finally, some engineers and designers feel that the psychological aspects of design are so complex that it is impractical even to try to cope with them. They argue that if all the possible factors that could go wrong were to be taken into account, the work system which would result would be so complicated that it would be practically impossible to build — even supposing it could be designed at a reasonable cost and within a reasonable period of time in the first place. The first point to make on this argument is that designing a safer work system does not mean becoming bogged down in a welter of detail as one tries to allow for all possible errors. Certainly it is desirable to reduce the likelihood of an error being made because errors waste time, introduce inefficiencies and are therefore costly. However, not all errors are critical for safety.

As noted repeatedly in this chapter, the key factor is to identify both the *safety critical scenario* and the *kind of error* that the operator is likely to make in relation to it. Once the error type has been identified, it should be possible to engineer its prevention or to allow for recovery from it and its effects. This approach to safety policy requires that the following related principles should be observed when designing or selecting equipment:

1.   The design team should be multi-disciplinary and should include opera-

tors as well as engineering and psychology professionals.[12] Experienced operators will have a view on the kinds of problems that can arise when a plant is running under normal and abnormal conditions. Their perspective can bring valuable insights to the design team that may shorten the period for commissioning and debugging the system as well as ensuring its safer operation over the long run.

2. Contextual factors should be taken into account in the design processes and should be included in operating specifications. When a piece of equipment for a manufacturing or service technology moves from the design and development stage to use in a workplace, factors other than technical questions arise. For example, we can ask whether the system can be operated without risk of critical errors being made by a fatigued operator at the end of a shift. We can ask whether there is a danger of cognitive overload if the organisation has a 'lean' staffing policy so that an operator may be required to monitor more information sources than working memory capacity will safely allow. We must also consider the organisation's culture. A culture which emphasises internal competition creates stress within its workforce. This will reduce their cognitive capacity (which will be devoted to managing the stress) and may increase the risks involved in operating a complex technical system.

It is worth repeating a point made earlier in Chapter 2. A system that is an adequate and even excellent technical achievement as an engineering concept may be seriously deficient and even dangerous in a particular work setting. It is not enough to select a technology that can do the job. It is essential to choose the technological option that will do the job effectively and safely in the context of the policies, procedures and culture of the particular organisation or company where it is to be used.

---

[12]Pidgeon, N. (1988) 'Risk Assessment and Accident Analysis' *Acta Psychologica*, 68, (1–3 Special Issue), pp.355–68; Warms-Ringdahl, L. (1987) 'Safety Analysis in Design: Evaluation of a Case Study', *Accident Analysis and Prevention*. 19, (4), pp. 305–17.

Chapter 7

Promoting Safer Working

From what has been said so far you can see that safety at work is a multi-dimensional issue. As we examined different aspects of the psychology of working safely, we noted a variety of steps that must be taken by organisations to create the conditions in which safer working becomes possible. Table 7.1 summarises these steps and the reasons for taking them.

Table 7.1: Steps to be taken to improve safety at work

Action	Reason
Note that insurance does not cover the ledger costs of accidents and ensure that staff understand this	Creates an awareness of the importance of safety, even in those who only think of 'the bottom line'
Take a broad band approach to incident/accident recording	To get as accurate a picture as possible of workplace risk
Use positive and negative feedback and good example to teach safer working habits	To overcome the effects of the accident–incident ratio triangle and to create a safer culture
Examine the interaction between the situation and the person in cases of accident repetition	To determine what action needs to be taken to reduce repetition and to avoid the fatalism of accident proneness thinking
Understand how people think about hazards and risk	To communicate better about workplace dangers
Understand how people process information	To design safer machinery, equipment and workplace systems by allowing for the limits of working memory, thinking biases etc.

Working safely is not *only* a matter for organisational policy, however. Individual people (irrespective of their position in the organisation) have an equally vital role. The organisation creates the *possibility* for safer working. It does this through its commitment to safety. People see and experience this commitment in tangible form in the policies, procedures and management practice of the organisation, and in the resources allocated to safety. Policies, procedures and management practice come to life (or don't) through the actions of the people who implement them and who actually deploy the resources available for safety. Individuals — managers, operators and support staff — must be committed to safety in their moment-to-moment behaviour in the workplace if safer working is to be a reality. The actuality of safety is a matter for the people who compose the organisation.

In this chapter we look at some ways of promoting commitment to safer working among the individuals and groups of individuals who make up the organisation. We begin by looking at strategies that can be used by policy makers to encourage the owners and managers of organisations to invest in safety. We then look at media based safety campaigns, behavioural techniques and finally at what I will call the human resource approach to safety promotion.

PROMOTING INVESTMENT IN SAFETY BY OWNERS AND MANAGERS

The fact that some owners and managers have little or no interest in working more safely was noted in Chapter 1. The view of people in this small but safety critical category is that safety is too costly and that really troublesome accidents are too infrequent for them to bother investing money and time in improving safety in their organisations. If the worst happens they believe that insurance will cover the cost. Figures showing that insurance does *not* cover the actual costs of a near miss or a workplace accident were given in Chapter 1. We also noted that a minority of employees share this narrow view of safety at work and emphasise the role of insurance in compensating them for the consequences of a work related accident. These employees overlook the hidden costs of living with chronic pain and/or restricted mobility and the effects of this, as well as of the initial trauma, on family members.

The *safety quality incentive* approach that I discuss in this section is aimed at addressing the problem of the lack of motivation to invest in safer working on the part of some employers and managers. It is based on the behavioural principles of reinforcement and is a modification of an economic incentive scheme to promote health and safety at work proposed by the European Foundation for the Improvement of Living and Working Conditions.[1]

For those who are not proactive in meeting the needs for greater safety at work, frequent inspections by the HSA, with enforcement of compliance with

---

[1] Bailey, S., Jorgensen, K., Koch, C., Kruger, W. and Litske. (1995) *An Innovative Economic Incentive Model for Improvement of the Working Environment in Europe*. Dublin: European Foundation for the Improvement of Living and Working Conditions.

regulations through the courts if necessary, is one course of action. It is crucial to the success of this enforcement approach that any sanctions imposed have a meaningful impact on the defaulter. Fines or other penalties which do not 'hurt' the delinquent owner or employer will not change that person's attitude to workplace safety. The safety quality incentive approach suggested here adds a carrot to this stick.

This scheme would involve awarding a publicly recognisable safety quality mark, similar to the Q mark or ISO award, to organisations that develop and implement technically, ergonomically and psychologically sound safety systems. Since standards tend to deteriorate over time, organisations should be required to reapply for the safety quality mark after a specified interval. Where several organisations offer the same kind and quality of product or service, but only one holds the safety quality mark, government offices and public companies would be required to deal with that organisation.

Some organisations argue that safety is so expensive that it makes them less competitive than a rival who cuts corners on safety. This factor could be dealt with by allowing organisations to offset provable cost increases resulting directly from taking safety seriously against corporation tax. The corporation tax system is a vehicle that could be used in any number of creative ways to support initiatives in the safety area at industry as well as organisational level. The details of such a scheme would obviously have to be carefully thought through. However, the rationale of encouraging owners and employers to promote safer working policies and practices by rewarding organisations for investing in safety is based on psychological principles that are known to work.

PROMOTING SAFER WORKING THROUGH MEDIA AND POSTER BASED CAMPAIGNS

Some safety campaigns are run by government or statutory bodies on a national basis through the media (e.g. anti-speeding campaigns), or are focused on a particular industry or group (e.g. safety in farming with posters and literature distributed through the HSA and farming organisations as well as in the public media). Such campaigns usually have one or more of the following aims:

• to raise awareness of an issue

• to inform about an issue

• to change attitudes and, eventually, behaviour regarding an issue.

Provided the target audience uses the medium through which the campaign is directed (i.e. people watch television when the advert is on or they read the

ad in the newspaper or the poster in their workplace), such campaigns probably succeed in achieving the aim of making the target group aware of an
issue. The extent to which they inform people about the issue and the extent
to which they influence people's attitudes and behaviours regarding it are
more questionable.

There are many reasons why the effectiveness of broad spectrum media
and poster campaigns cannot be assured. Some of the principal ones, which
relate to how individuals think about and react to safety and risk related information, are as follows:

1. The content does not appear to be *relevant* to them, even though they are
    members of the target group. For example, in Chapter 5 we saw that
    people tend to overestimate their level of skill in car driving. As a result,
    people who drive too fast may exclude themselves as the target of an
    anti-speed campaign because they believe only less skilled drivers are
    dangerous and should drive more slowly.

2. The members of the target group do not believe in the effectiveness of
    the proposed safety method. For example, an employee may not believe
    that protective gloves will really be effective in guarding his hands in the
    event of an acid spill.

3. Some or all of the members of the target group have a fatalistic attitude
    to safety — that is, they have an external locus of control regarding safety.
    (Locus of control was discussed in Chapter 4.) Because some people
    believe that accidents "just happen", they will not be inclined to act on
    the basis of information given in the campaign.

4. Some people react defensively to threat and to being informed of risk.
    They may stop processing the information once they realise it is about a
    threatening or unpleasant subject. They may avoid further exposure to it
    (e.g. by going out of the room when the adverts come on, turning down
    the sound or reading or talking until the ads are over). They may ques-
    tion the truth of the information given or question the reliability and
    expertise of the source of the information — "Those so-called experts
    have one story this week but they'll be telling us the opposite in a month".

The last point relates to the complex question of whether or not fear is an
effective means of producing attitude and behaviour change. The research
shows that for fear to be effective, the campaign material must also give
information on how the person can change or otherwise deal with the dangerous situation or behaviour.[2] If it doesn't, people will simply be made to

---

[2] Leventhal, H., Watts, J. C. and Pagano, F. (1967) 'Effects of Fear and Instructions
on How to Cope with Danger', *Journal of Personality and Social Psychology.* 6,
pp.313–21.

feel helpless. They may then react by becoming panic-stricken, or may become angry and/or cynical towards the source (person or agency) which has increased their anxiety without showing them a way out. As noted above, another form of reacting is to tune out the information that causes the fear and avoid exposure to it in the future.

IMPROVING THE EFFECTIVENESS OF MEDIA AND POSTER CAMPAIGNS

From what has just been said, it will be evident to you that these kinds of campaigns can have a large margin of error in their ability to hit their target effectively and produce a change in attitude and behaviour. While their effectiveness can never be 100% assured, some steps can be taken to increase the likelihood of their message getting through to and influencing a target group. In brief, these steps are:

• focus the campaign on a specific target group rather than designing a more broadly based, general campaign

• make sure that the issues covered in the campaign, and the style and format in which they are presented, take account of the perspective of the target group or groups on those issues

• make sure that the material used in the campaign includes information on how the hazard can be removed or avoided, and/or on how people can work more safely on the job

• link safer working to attractive non-safety aspects of the job, e.g. professionalism

• take account of cognitive biases when preparing and presenting information.

Let us look at each of these points in more detail.

Focus the campaign

Broad spectrum, general campaigns on safety promotion (or indeed on any issue) allow too much scope for people to dismiss the message as irrelevant to themselves. We noted earlier in this chapter, and in the discussion of how people perceive risk in Chapter 5, that individuals tend to see themselves as exceptions to the rule. For example, an experienced lab technician may believe that she is so skilled at this point that she can ignore regulations which "... are really only there for junior staff just in the door". A campaign focused precisely on a specific target group will be more likely to grab their attention. The likelihood of this happening will be increased if the content of the campaign and the way it is presented take account of the perspective of the target group. In this regard it may be necessary to think about the placing and timing of campaign material. Researchers recommend that posters should be displayed near the location of the safety issue in question.[3] For example, a poster about forklift truck safety should be placed in the forklift truck bay and not in the canteen. Likewise, a TV ad advocating care when carrying out electrical repairs at work is probably not well timed if it appears during the evening meal when people are 'switched off' from work and are focussed on relaxing with the family.

Choosing and presenting the issues

We noted at the end of Chapter 5 that the perspectives of safety experts and of non-experts can differ — sometimes quite radically. This means that laypeople may not see as dangerous aspects of the situation or of their own behaviour which in statistical terms really are hazards. On the other hand, safety experts may discount features of the job or the work situation that cause very real concern to the employees involved. If the content of the safety campaign does not address the issues that cause concern to the target group, the campaign as a whole will be seen as irrelevant and will be ignored. Similarly, if the issues which experts see as critical for safety are not presented and discussed in a way which takes account of the reasons why laypeople do *not* see them as hazardous, the campaign will fail. Planning the campaign should include discussions with a representative sample of the target group so that the content and presentation format of the campaign will be tailored to the psychology of the group. The focus group technique is a useful way of discovering the views of a target group. The technique uses carefully thought out questions to guide the discussion of the topic by the group.[4]

Be constructive

The third element in making safety campaigns more effective is to give information on working safely. We noted earlier that simply warning about the dangers involved in particular situations or behaviours without also giving information on how the hazard can be removed or avoided, or on how a task can be done more safely, is ineffective in promoting attitude and behaviour change. Messages that *only* create fear and anxiety will be avoided or discounted in some way by those who see or hear them. The warning poster may be torn down or defaced — black humour is one way of dealing with anxiety.

---

[3] Sell, R.G. (1977) 'What Does Safety Propaganda do for Safety? A Review', *Applied Ergonomics*. 8, (4), pp. 203–14.

[4] For a discussion of focus groups see Krueger, Richard A. (1994) *Focus Groups: A Practical Guide for Applied Research*. London: Sage Publications.

We noted earlier that calling the credibility of the source of the warning into question is another way of reacting when one is made anxious but is not shown a way of dealing with the problem. Where the campaign message itself does not include sufficient material to help the person to make the changes in behaviour that the campaign calls for, it should always include information on sources to which the individual can go for such help.

Link to the positive

Charles Hampden-Turner[5] describes a case study at an American oil company where a culture of safety was created among the truckers by emphasising the special knowledge that they had about the hazards involved in transporting gasoline by road. Campaign material that refers to attractive, non-safety aspects of the job, such as the professionalism and skill of the person who works safely, makes the campaign more interesting and gives people a reason for acting proactively and positively rather than just defensively.[6]

Taking account of the cognitive biases

The cognitive biases discussed in Chapter 5 should be taken into account when preparing and presenting safety information for the campaign. The imaginability bias would suggest that campaign material showing the outcome of unsafe behaviour in concrete and personal terms will have more impact on the audience than more abstract material, such as statistical data. Thus, material showing an accident victim in a wheelchair with a sentence or two from a family member describing the impact which the accident has had on their lives could be used to get a safety message across. A photograph of a grieving child would have a similar emotional impact. (Of course this should be used in the context of giving the employees information on how to avoid injury.) Anchoring bias (the effect on how information is framed when first presented on the subsequent perception of the risk in the situation) suggests that emphasis on more frequent events will increase our awareness of workplace hazards than will emphasis on infrequent events, even if these

---

[5] Hampden-Turner, C. (1990) 'Western Oil: A Culture of Safety' in Chapter 3 of *Corporate Culture: From Vicious to Virtuous Circles*. London: The Economist Books and Hutchinson Business Books Ltd.

[6] It will probably have struck you that this point involves *a reversal* of the situation described by Pirani and Reynolds referred to in Chapter 5. There we saw that managers and co-workers can have a negative view of someone who is concerned with safety. Hampden-Turner's case study shows that this does not have to be the case if we emphasise skill and professionalism rather than an individualistic 'macho' culture.

latter are fatal. It is also worthwhile remembering that for some people death may not be feared as much as severe disability such as paralysis.[7]

In general

These kinds of safety campaigns should be special events. They should be time limited and should address just a few key factors in a way that gets attention and gives information. Leaving posters up until they become shabby and torn detracts from the impact of their message. In addition, the importance of safety at work as a general issue for concern is undermined when people are allowed to habituate to and thus take for granted any one part of it. A two or three week campaign,[8] carefully focused on a topic selected for its relevance to a particular group and presented in a way which links safety to the concerns of that group, stands the best chance of increasing awareness of safety issues among its members. This will at least create the conditions for attitude and behaviour change.

BEHAVIOURAL TECHNIQUES FOR PROMOTING SAFER WORKING

The key psychological concepts which underpin behavioural techniques for promoting safer working[9] were discussed in detail in Chapter 3. In that chapter the dynamics of learning and behaviour change were described in broad terms so that managers and safety professionals could see the necessity for creating an organisational culture with a clear and consistent commitment to working safely. In this section we focus again on the principles of learning, but this time we do so from the point of view of their systematic application in a programme designed to modify a specific instance or case of unsafe behaviour. Among the kinds of safety related behaviours which have been improved using behavioural techniques are:

- wearing car seatbelts

- driving more carefully in an urban setting

---

[7] Green, C. H. and Brown, R. A. (1978) *The Acceptability of Risk: Summary Report.* Boram Wood, Fire Research Station.

[8] R.G. Sell notes that the British Safety Council recommends that posters should only remain up for ten working days. This seems too short a period to make an impact, given that most safety professionals advise using posters to supplement an 'in-house' training and discussion programme on the issues covered in the campaign. Posters should be displayed for a period after the programme to remind people of it and to reinforce its message.

[9] Bird, F. E. and Schlesinger, L. E. (1970) 'Safe Behaviour Reinforcement', *Journal of the American Society for Safety Engineers.* June, pp. 16–24.

- wearing ear protection

- wearing safety glasses.[10]

Safety promotion strategies which systematically use the principles of learning to modify a specific instance of unsafe behaviour involve three elements. These three elements are known as the *ABC* of behaviour change — for reasons which will become obvious to you in a moment. The **A** element refers to the **A**ntecedent conditions which form the context for the **B**ehaviour which we are interested in changing. The Antecedent, or setting, conditions may involve the physical environment in which the Behaviour takes place. They may involve an interpersonal situation such as a group of people working together where there is competition between some members of the group to complete the task before the others. The point to note about the Antecedent conditions from the safety perspective is that they tend to be a *cue* for unsafe **B**ehaviour or risk taking on the part of the people involved.

The **C** element refers to the **C**onsequence or outcome which follows the Behaviour. In 1987 Beth Sulzer-Azaroff[11] noted that Consequences which are most likely to lead to an action being repeated follow the person's Behaviour immediately each time it takes place and are positively valued by the person. In other words, Consequences which are most effective in influencing Behaviour are those which are *soon*, *certain* and *positive*.

Programmes of safety promotion based on behavioural techniques begin by identifying precisely what unsafe Behaviour is to be eliminated. The Behaviour is monitored so that its Antecedent conditions and the Consequences that currently follow it and maintain it are noted. The safety professional then looks for ways to change the Consequences that follow the unsafe Behaviour so that they are no longer reinforcing it. In tandem with this, he will put in place a clear alternative Behaviour which has positive Consequences for the person, but which is safe to do. An example of this kind of programme is given in Table 7.2

Safety promotion programmes based on behaviour modification principles have been used in a wide variety of settings over the years.[12] Research studies of their effectiveness suggest that incentives such as trading stamps, free bus passes, dinners for the employees and their partners, money and bonus vacation time are effective reinforcers for safer behaviour at work.

---

[10]McAfee, R. B. and Winn, A. R. (1989) 'The Use of Incentives/Feedback to Enhance Work Place safety: A Critique of the Literature', *Journal of Safety Research*. 20, pp. 7–19.

[11]Sulzer-Azeroff, B. (1987) 'The Modification of Occupational Safety Behaviour', *Journal of Occupational Accidents*. 9, pp. 177–97.

[12]Peters, R. H. (1991) 'Strategies for Encouraging Self-Protective Employee Behaviour', *Journal of Safety Research*. 22, pp. 53–70.

Table 7.2: Example of a behaviour based safety intervention

Observation period	Antecedent	Behaviour	Consequences
Baseline (pre-programme)	Time cued —unsafe behaviour takes place only during last 30–45 minutes of a shift (prior to clocking out)	Not wearing safety glasses. Practice has developed of a member of the shift taking everyone's glasses to the store before end of shift	Getting away more quickly at the end of the shift. Staff had only to clock out and not go to the store
Intervention (implementation of behavioural programme)	During critical time period, remind staff of requirement to wear safety glasses	Compliance with regulation	Arranging to have glasses collected at clock and taken to store by stores person. Operating staff are not delayed by the need to take glasses to store themselves

Less tangible consequences, such as feedback on performance combined with goal setting and praise and written acknowledgement of improved safety performance were as effective, and in many cases had even more impact on behaviour than extrinsic rewards.

The principal weakness in the strict behavioural approach to promoting safer working centres around the instability of the behaviour once the programme is withdrawn. This is particularly likely to happen when the consequences are tangible reinforcers, such as bonus payments or holidays, or rewards such as household appliances. In the case of bonus payments or additional vacation time, these can come to be seen as part of the employee's remuneration or conditions of employment. As a result, any attempt to withdraw or reduce them for poor safety performance can be greatly resented.

Behavioural techniques are probably best used to *launch* a safety initiative. Thereafter they could be used very occasionally to focus attention on a specific safety problem. The finding that goal setting and feedback is as effective as more tangible reinforcers in producing safer behaviour puts the spotlight on that much misunderstood and underestimated side of commercial life — the human resource.

THE HUMAN RESOURCE APPROACH TO SAFETY PROMOTION

This approach to promoting safer working starts from the position that the *human resource* involves not only the hands but also the heads and hearts of the people who make up the workforce of an organisation. This view sees the intelligence and commitment of personnel as a resource as valuable to an enterprise as the financial capital, plant and equipment that the organisation possesses.[13] The human resource approach assumes that the people involved in doing a job will have useful information on safety related aspects of the design and operation of the equipment used, the layout of the workplace, workflow arrangements and so forth. This store of first-hand information is drawn on by the safety professional who works with the members of the work group to improve safety in the workplace.

Involving employees in safety planning in their area has two major benefits:

1. It increases the likelihood that the steps taken are addressing real operational hazards in that workplace.

2. It increases the likelihood that any safety measures put in place will be followed by the members of the work group involved since they will have had a role in deciding on them.

Research on attitude and behaviour change shows that people are more likely to be committed to a course of action that they have had a part in deciding[14] and of which they feel 'ownership'. There is also research to show that we are more likely to follow through on a commitment that we have made in public.[15] We usually seek to avoid the state of dissonance or tension and critical self-evaluation that would arise if we were to behave in a way that contradicts our stated public position.[16]

The human resource approach to safety promotion capitalises on the psychological situation just described. It uses the experience and insight of those doing the job to ensure that the hazards planned for include those actually involved in doing the job. By acknowledging and taking into account the

---

[13]The related ideas of human capital, 'knowledge-as-capital' and the 'knowledge economy' have been written about for a number of years but have still to make an impact on the structure and function of most organisations and economies. See Crawford, R. (1991) *In the Era of Human Capital*, Harper Business.

[14]Furnham, A. (1997) *The Psychology of Behaviour At Work*. Hove: The Psychology Press and Taylor & Francis. (Section on motivation enhancing techniques in chapter 6.)

[15]Deutch, M. and Gerard, H. B. (1955) 'A Study of Normative and Informational Social Influence upon Individual Judgement', *Journal of Abnormal and Social Psychology*. 51, pp. 629–36. Katzev, R. and Wang, T. (1994) 'Can Commitment Change Behaviour? A Case Study of Environmental Actions', *Journal of Social Behaviour and Personality*. 9, pp. 13–26.

[16]Aronson, E. (1997) 'The Theory of Cognitive Dissonance: The Evolution and Vicissitudes of an Idea' In C. McGarty and S.A. Haslam (Eds). *The Message of Social Psychology*. Oxford: Blackwell.

experience and expertise of the workforce, the safety professional is giving the employees part-ownership of the safety procedures which emerge from discussion with them. The psychological dice is then loaded more in the direction of a greater commitment by personnel to following procedures and making the safety plan work than would be the case if the plan was imposed from outside. This approach does not mean that the contribution of systems designers, engineers and safety experts is ignored. Rather than valuing the knowledge of one group to the exclusion of the insights of the other, the human resource view draws on *all* possible sources of relevant information. By working together both experts and operatives can gain a better understanding of each other's perspectives. This will ultimately lead to a narrowing of the safety communication gap between experts and laypeople. It should be noted that this joint approach to safety can bring the added bonus of creating a climate of greater understanding, mutual respect and trust among those involved. This can lay a foundation on which other human resource and organisational development initiatives, such as team building and a partnership approach to operating the enterprise as a whole, can be based.

IN CONCLUSION

It is usual to talk about safety promotion in terms of three strategies — engineering, education, and enforcement. One of the aims of this book was to explain the nature of human resources more fully. People are not machines but, like machines, they do function in particular ways. If we are to work more safely we need to understand how people function so that we can *engineer* systems which are compatible with the psychological nature of the people who are to use them.

The capacity to *learn* (education) is one of our unique features as the human resource. We constantly seek to understand our environment and what is going on around us. Where we are not given clear and full information on this, we will create our own schemas and stories to make sense of our observations and experience. If these schemas and stories are not accurate, serious problems may arise for the organisation due to misunderstandings and misperceptions. *Educating* employees by opening up discussion on the kinds of issues covered in the various chapters of this book will capitalise on our learning ability.

Enforcement can be looked at as consistency in sticking to and implementing the organisation's safety policy. Never turning a blind eye to unsafe behaviour and leading by example means that enforcement as such will rarely need to be resorted to in its negative or punishing sense.

In this final chapter I have added another element to the trio of engineering, education and enforcement. This fourth element is *involvement*. Actively *involving* employees at all levels as collaborators in developing safer policies, procedures and practices at work means that we are really seeing people as a *resource* within the organisation. The insights which employees at all levels have that are relevant to working safely are drawn on, and commitment to safer working is created when safety is made everybody's business and not just the sole responsibility of management or safety advisors and representatives.

Index